MENSA

— PRESENTS —

MIND MAZES

— for —

KIDS

Text copyright © 1995 British Mensa Limited
Design and artwork copyright © 1995 Carlton Books Limited

This edition published by Carlton Books Limited 1999

A CIP catalogue for this book is available from the British Library

ISBN 1-85868-140-5

Designed by Neil Jeffreys

Printed in Italy

MENSA
PRESENTS

MIND MAZES for KIDS

Robert Allen

CARLTON

CONTENTS

Let's face it, just about anyone can solve puzzles. Yes, some of them might be a bit tricky but, given enough time, you'll probably get the answer. So we thought you might like to try something a little different. Something just a bit more taxing. Something, in fact, that will reduce your brain cells to the consistency of marshmallow. What is it? A Mind Maze, that's what! In fact, nine mazes that increase in difficulty as you work your way through the book. Each maze is an ingeniously constructed instrument of mental torture – a series of cunningly linked puzzles in which even a single mistake can prove fatal. The early ones are only 15 puzzles long but, even if you survive these, you will find that you then have to solve mazes of 25 puzzles, and finally, a 40-puzzle monster maze. So don't just sit there – you have a lot of solving to do.

If you like puzzles, you'll like Mensa. The high-IQ society is the only club in the world exclusively for people with a talent for puzzle solving. If you'd like to know more then either contact British Mensa Limited, Dept CB, St John's Square, Wolverhampton WV2 4AH, England, or contact your national Mensa at Mensa International, 15 The Ivories, 628 Northampton Street, London N1 2HY, England.

R. P. Allen

Robert Allen
Editorial Director
Mensa Publications

In each maze the puzzles are linked in a certain order which is quite different from their numerical order in the book. The answer to each puzzle is constructed in such a way that it guides you to the next one in the series. For example, let's take a puzzle like this:

PUZZLE 1

Find the number in this series. When you have the answer, double it and go to the next puzzle.

2   4   6   8   10   ?

The series increases by two at each step, so the number to replace the question mark is 12. You then double it to make 24 and *that* is the number of the next puzzle you should attempt.

Quite often in these mazes we use letters instead of numbers. To help you we have used only one system for conversion: a simple substitution based on alphabetical position, so that, for example, A = 1, B = 2, ... M = 13, N = 14, ... Z = 26.

The Little-Bickering-in-the-Marsh Motor Club is having its annual Treasure Hunt. Contestants have to drive from one site to another solving the clues as they go. You only win if you visit all the locations in the correct order.

PUZZLE 1

Can you find the missing letter? You might discover it in a far-off land. If you think the answer is J, go to 6. If you choose A, go to 5. If you choose O, go to 12.

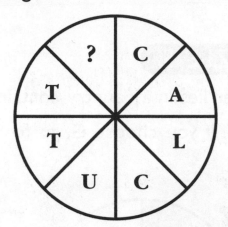

PUZZLE 2

Danielle travels around Europe. She likes Paris, but not London. She likes Frankfurt but not Bonn. She likes Amsterdam, but not Barcelona. Oh, does she like St Petersburg? If you choose Yes, go to 15. If you choose No, go to 8.

PUZZLE 3

Find the missing letter. If you choose B, go to 6. If you choose F, go to 11. If you choose O, go to 14.

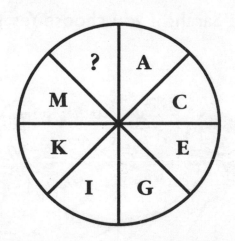

PUZZLE 4

The following letters all have a numerical value. If the word TEA is worth 4, and TEAS is worth 8, what would SEATS be worth? When you have the answer subtract 2 and go to the next location.

PUZZLE 5

Find the missing letter. The answer lies in a country containing two islands. If you choose D, go to 7. If you choose G, go to 9. If you choose E, go to 8.

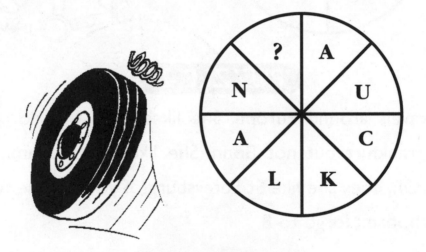

PUZZLE 6

Suzy goes to a new school. In her class she likes Fred but doesn't like Graham. She likes Ross but doesn't like Anna. She likes Mandy but doesn't like Sandra. Does she like Sarah? If you choose Yes, go to 2. If you choose No, go to 11.

PUZZLE 7

Dale wins a tour of the USA. He likes Arizona, but hates Texas. He likes Nebraska, but hates Massachusetts. He likes Maine, but hates Minnesota. Does he like Indiana? If you choose Yes, go to 13. If you choose No, go to 15.

PUZZLE 8

Find the missing number? When you have the number, halve it and go to the next location.

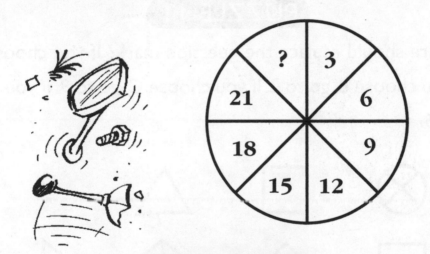

PUZZLE 9

Find the missing number. When you have the answer subtract 33 and go to the next location.

PUZZLE 10

Find the missing number. When you have the answer add 1 and go to the next location.

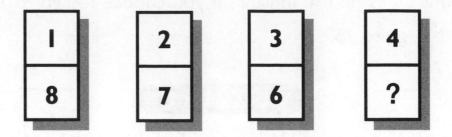

PUZZLE 11

Which figure should replace the question mark? If you choose A, go to 14. If you choose B, go to 2. If you choose C, go to 9. If you choose D, go to 16.

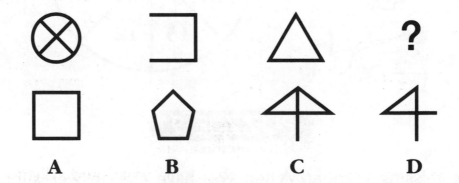

PUZZLE 12

Which of the following is the odd one out?

a) HOCNIP b) TEVEHENOB c) ZOMRAT d) NICLNOT

If you choose a), go to 14. If you choose b), go to 4. If you choose c), go to 10. If you choose d), go to 3.

PUZZLE 13

Find the missing letter. You may find you need the aid of a man of genius. If you choose F, go to 4. If you choose S, go to 6. If you choose N, go to 2.

PUZZLE 14

Find the missing letter. If you think it's K, go to 6. If you choose F, go to 4. If you choose I, go to 9.

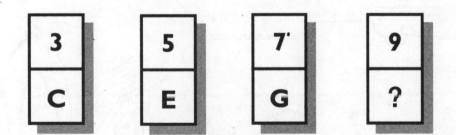

PUZZLE 15

Find the missing letter. Look for someone small and "digital". If you choose B, go to 8. If you choose R, go to 14. If you choose A, go to 11.

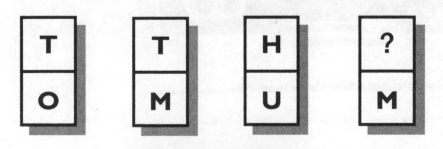

PUZZLE 16

Welcome to the finish. What was your path?

This is a test paper for entry as Cadet Commander of the Intergalactic Federation. Candidates have half a Terran hour to complete the Maze.

PUZZLE 1

The letters in this square form a simple sequence. Find the one needed to replace the question mark. If you choose D, go to 12. If you choose S, go to 13. If you choose A, go to 9.

J	F	M
J	M	A
J	A	?

PUZZLE 2

The numbers in each sector of the wheel are linked in some way. Find the number needed to replace the question mark. When you have the number, add 3 and go to the next location.

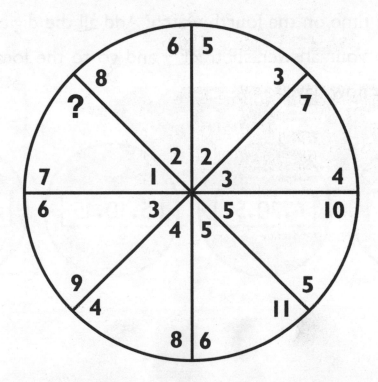

MAZE 2

PUZZLE 3

The numbers and letters in this square are linked. Find the correct number to replace the question mark. It will help if you think of the alphabet laid out in a circle, rather than a straight line. When you have the answer, double it and go the next location.

A	5	G
?		7
T	4	O

PUZZLE 4

What is the time on the fourth watch? Add all the digits (*not* whole numbers) in your answer, subtract 9 and go to the location whose number you now have.

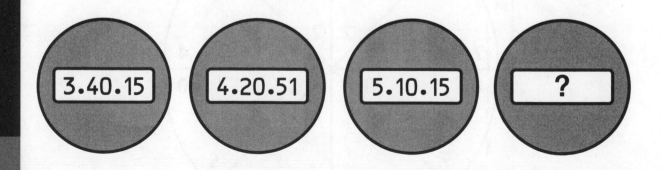

3.40.15   4.20.51   5.10.15   ?

PUZZLE 5

Find the missing number. When you have the number, subtract 17 and go to the next location.

$$\frac{3 \mid 6}{24 \mid 12} \qquad \frac{2 \mid 4}{16 \mid 8} \qquad \frac{1 \mid 2}{8 \mid 4} \qquad \frac{5 \mid 10}{40 \mid ?}$$

PUZZLE 6

Which is the missing number? When you have it add 6 and go the next location.

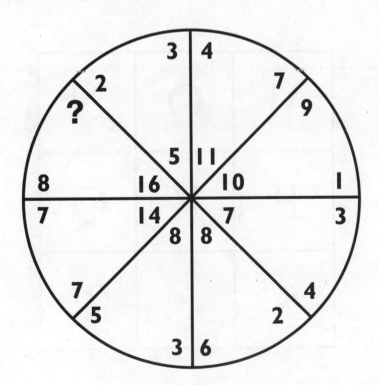

PUZZLE 7

Which figure is the odd one out? If you choose A, go to 8. If you choose B, go to 6. If you choose C, go to 15. If you choose D, go to 10.

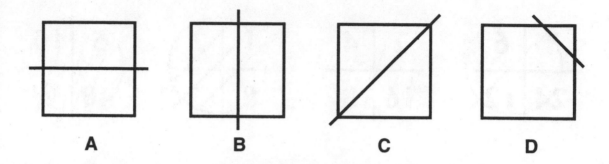

A   B   C   D

PUZZLE 8

Find the missing letter. If you choose K, go to 9. If you choose U, go to 15. If you choose J, go to 3.

M	O	N
P	R	Q
S	?	T

PUZZLE 9

Which circle is the odd one out? If you choose A, go to 4. If you choose B, go to 6. If you choose C, go to 7. If you choose D, go to 10.

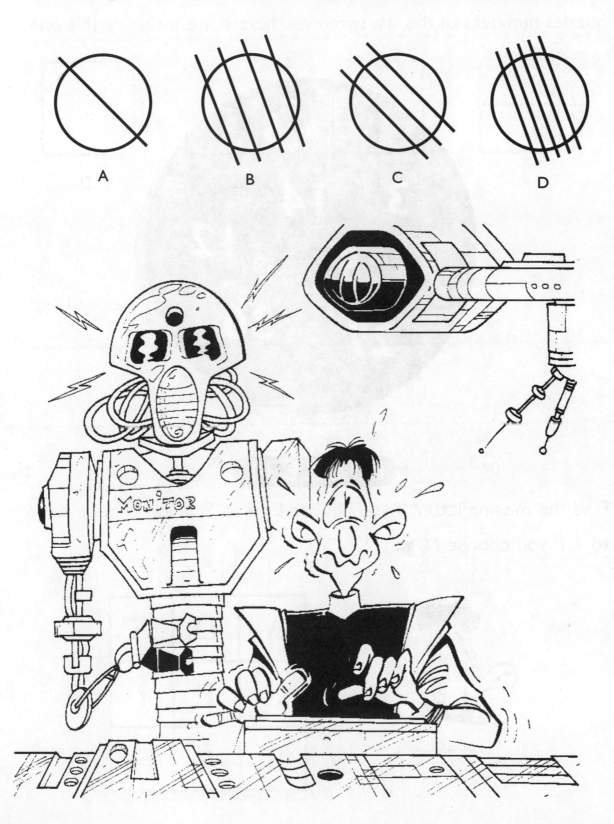

A   B   C   D

MAZE 2

PUZZLE 10

Which is the odd number out? You have now almost completed the examination. To pass, however, you will need to add together the puzzles numbers of the last seven you have done, including this one.

PUZZLE 11

Find the missing letter. If you choose I, go to 5. If you choose K, go to 7. If you choose N, go to 2.

A	D	G
C	F	?
B	E	H

PUZZLE 12

Which letter is the odd one out? When you have the answer, convert it into a number using the system A = 1, B = 2, etc. Then subtract 4 and go to the next location.

PUZZLE 13

The letters in this square, when read in the correct order, spell the name of a famous author. What is the missing letter? If you choose K, go to 4. If you choose W, go to 14. If you choose C, go to 12. If you choose H, go to 11.

M	W	A
A	T	I
R	?	N

PUZZLE 14

Which word is in the wrong circle? When you have the right word, take its first letter and, using the system A = 1, B = 2 etc., convert it into a number. You now have the number of the next location.

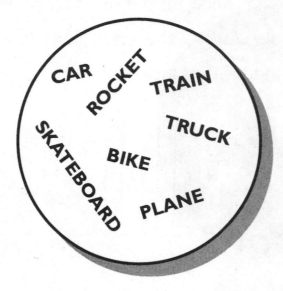

PUZZLE 15

Which item in the right-hand box could logically appear in the left-hand box? If you choose Car, go to 11. If you choose Clock, go to 14. If you choose Window, go to 10. If you choose Sesame, go to 11. If you choose Piano, go to 12.

APPLE	CAR
WHEAT	CLOCK
EGG	WINDOW
SUGAR	SESAME
PIZZA	PIANO

You are a secret agent. Your job is to break into the enemy HQ, open the safe, and extract the secret plans. However, you find a small complication awaits you. The combination of the safe is guarded by a series of fiendish puzzles that form a Mind Maze. You must press the buttons strictly in the order dictated by the maze. One false move and the whole thing will explode. Good luck!

PUZZLE 1

Which of these figures is the odd one out? If you choose A, go to 14. If you choose B, go to 5. If you choose C, go to 7. If you choose D, go to 8.

A   B   C   D

PUZZLE 2

In an office of 180 people the canteen offers a choice of Lasagne, Vegetable Curry, and Gammon Steak Hawaii. On Tuesday 60 people chose Lasagne, and two-thirds chose the Gammon Steak Hawaii. How many chose Vegetable Curry? When you have the answer, add 15 and go to the next location.

PUZZLE 3

If A x B = 48 and A − B = 8, what are the values of A and B? Now take three-quarters of A and go to that number.

PUZZLE 4

A man travels to work by bike, bus and on foot each day. If he travels 5 miles by bike, double that distance by bus, and walks a distance equal to one-tenth of the bus journey, how far will he travel in total? Now subtract 3 and go to the next puzzle.

PUZZLE 5

Find the missing number. When you have the answer, add 1 and go to the puzzle whose number you now have.

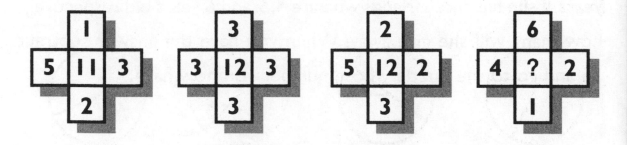

PUZZLE 6

The letters in this star form a familiar series. Which letter should go in the middle? If you choose B, go to 2. If you choose S, go to 11. If you choose M, go to 5.

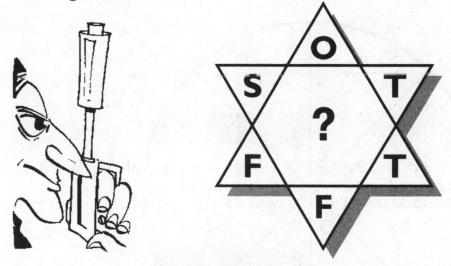

PUZZLE 7

If a man solves 6 puzzles each day, how many weeks will it take him to work his way through a magazine containing 84 puzzles. When you have the number add 10 and go to the next location.

PUZZLE 8

A little girl shares out her chocolates so that each of her friends is given a number of chocolates equal to three times his or her age in years. If she has three friends who are 4, 5, and 6 years old respectively, how many will she give away? When you have the answer subtract 35 and go to the puzzle whose number you now have.

PUZZLE 9

The numbers in this circle obey a simple formula. Can you discover what it is and replace the question mark with a number? Now subtract 5 and go to the next location.

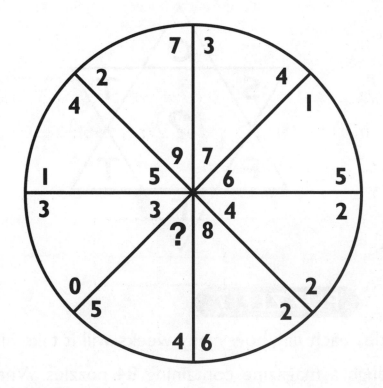

PUZZLE 10

What comes next in the series 7, 14, 21, 28… ? When you have the answer subtract 33 and go to the next location.

PUZZLE 11

This square has one strange quality. Discover what it is and then replace the question mark with a number. When you have the number add 5 and go to the next location.

5	5	0
4	3	3
1	?	7

PUZZLE 12

Can you solve the logic behind this diagram and find the missing letter? When you have, turn to the answers, because this is the end of the maze.

A	E	I
A	U	O
E	I	?

PUZZLE 13

Find the missing number. When you have it, subtract 14 and go to the next location.

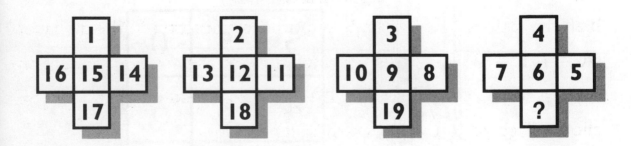

PUZZLE 14

Which of these crates is the odd one out? If you choose A, go to 13. If you choose B, go to 11. If you choose C, go to 3.

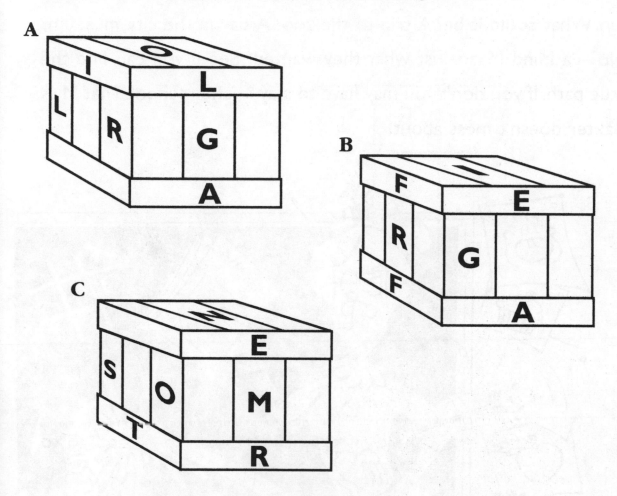

PUZZLE 15

If all the letters have values based on their position in the alphabet (A = 1, Z = 26 etc.), what is the value of the following equation expressed as a letter? J x R ÷ I = ? If you choose K, go to 7. If you choose T, go to 5. If you choose N, go to 12.

Miss Baxter was the new teacher of Class 2B. Before breaking for the summer vacation, she told them they were going to have some fun. What could it be? A trip to the zoo? A day in the city museum? No – a Mind Maze. Just what they wanted! See if you can find the true path. If you don't you may have to stay in after school. That Miss Baxter doesn't mess about!

PUZZLE 1

Hidden in the grid you will find the names of 10 American States. All are in a straight line, but some are written vertically, some horizontally and the remainder diagonally. How many of them are written vertically? Double your answer and go to the next location. The States are: Alabama, Arizona, California, Georgia, Indiana, Kansas, Maine, Mississippi, Oklahoma and Texas.

M	I	S	S	I	S	S	I	P	P	I	T	V	I	U	N
G	H	K	I	K	T	V	S	M	A	C	Q	R	N	T	K
C	B	A	L	R	X	O	T	Z	S	P	N	H	D	J	L
B	B	N	C	T	I	T	K	V	B	A	L	P	I	A	R
C	K	S	D	E	E	Q	B	L	P	S	R	S	A	C	I
B	O	A	B	X	E	D	I	R	A	G	I	A	N	N	T
C	A	S	S	A	B	D	R	O	A	H	V	B	A	N	T
D	V	W	Q	S	R	T	M	I	H	J	O	L	R	T	B
M	A	I	N	E	B	V	N	N	T	Q	P	M	L	H	C
X	I	C	R	S	B	R	P	C	I	R	A	M	A	R	C
A	U	D	R	A	O	R	E	P	D	E	O	M	O	R	D
A	D	A	T	F	E	R	I	A	R	I	Z	O	N	A	S
S	I	W	I	T	D	E	T	U	L	O	V	N	O	C	K
T	E	L	D	H	G	E	O	R	G	I	A	A	R	D	T
Y	A	T	I	X	E	L	P	M	O	C	D	A	E	R	O
C	E	N	I	G	M	D	P	A	L	A	B	A	M	A	Q

PUZZLE 2

In a secret code based on a 3 x 3 grid system each box of the grid contains three letters, as shown in the diagram below.

A B C	D E F	G H I
J K L	M N O	P Q R
S T U	V W X	Y Z

Use these clues to translate the following symbols. They will tell you which puzzle to attempt next.

PUZZLE 3

What is two-thirds of one-third? If your answer is one-third, go to 7. If your answer is one quarter, go to 14. If your answer is two-ninths, go to 7.

PUZZLE 4

If B + A = 10, and A − B = 6, what are the values of B and A? Add 9 to the value of B and go to the puzzle of that number.

PUZZLE 5

The symbols in this grid have been drawn in a certain sequence, starting top left. When you have worked out what it is you should be able to decide which of the boxes below would correctly fit in the blank space. If you choose A, go to 10. If you choose B, go to 2. If you choose C, go to 14. If you choose D, go to 11.

+	−	X	÷	+	−	X	÷	+	−	X	÷	+	−	X	÷
÷	X	−	+	÷	X	−	+	÷	X	−	+	÷	X	−	+
+	−	X	÷	+	−	X	÷	+	−	X	÷	+	−	X	÷
÷	X	−	+	÷	X	−	+	÷	X	−	+	÷	X	−	+
+	−	X	÷	+	−	X	÷	+	−	X	÷	+	−	X	÷
÷	X	−	+				+	÷	X	−	+	÷	X	−	+
+	−	X	÷				÷	+	−	X	÷	+	−	X	÷
÷	X	−	+				+	÷	X	−	+	÷	X	−	+
+	−	X	÷	+	−	X	÷	+	−	X	÷	+	−	X	÷
÷	X	−	+	÷	X	−	+	÷	X	−	+	÷	X	−	+
+	−	X	÷	+	−	X	÷	+	−	X	÷	+	−	X	÷
÷	X	−	+	÷	X	−	+	÷	X	−	+	÷	X	−	+
+	−	X	÷	+	−	X	÷	+	−	X	÷	+	−	X	÷
÷	X	−	+	÷	X	−	+	÷	X	−	+	÷	X	−	+
+	−	X	÷	+	−	X	÷	+	−	X	÷	+	−	X	÷
÷	X	−	+	÷	X	−	+	÷	X	−	+	÷	X	−	+

A

+	÷	−
X	÷	+
−	X	÷

B

−	X	÷
X	−	+
−	÷	X

C

÷	X	−
+	−	X
÷	X	−

D

+	+	X
−	÷	+
+	X	÷

PUZZLE 6

If two apples are needed to make an apple cake, and there are four apples to a kilo, how many cakes can be made from 5 kilos of apples? Go to the puzzle whose number you now have.

PUZZLE 7

At a birthday party half the guests drink cola, a quarter have lemonade, a sixth have orange juice, and the remaining three have water. How many guests were at the party? Add the digits of your answer together and subtract 4. Now go to the next location.

PUZZLE 8

Can you unravel the logic of these squares and find the missing number? Take two-thirds of the answer and go to the next puzzle.

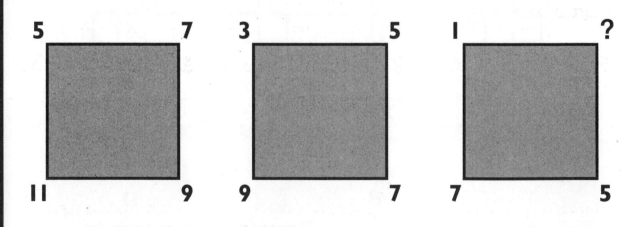

PUZZLE 9

These triangles have been numbered using a certain logic. When you have worked out what it is you will discover which number can correctly replace the question mark. Subtract 2 and go to the next puzzle.

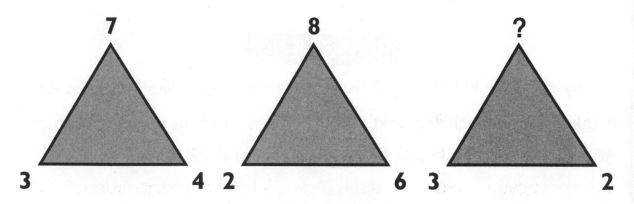

PUZZLE 10

This may look just like a puzzle you have seen elsewhere in this maze, but this time the logic is different! What number replaces the question mark? Subtract four from your answer and go to the next puzzle.

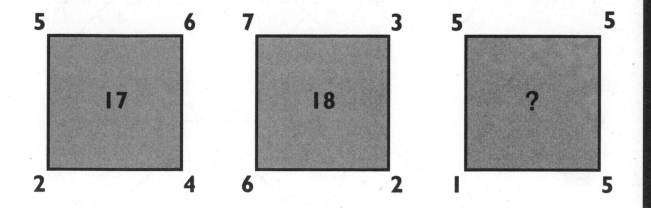

PUZZLE 11

If you write the alphabet in a circle, which letter would be nine places backward from F? If you choose X, go to 2. If you choose W, go to 8. If you choose T, go to 14.

PUZZLE 12

A boy rides his bicycle at 12 miles per hour. How many minutes will it take him to reach the next village, 9 miles from his house? Subtract 30 from your answer and go to the next location.

PUZZLE 13

Can you replace the question mark with a number in this circle? Double your answer and go to the next puzzle.

PUZZLE 14

If A = 13, B = 3A, and C = A + B, what is the value of C? This is the end of the maze. When you have worked this out, turn to the answers to see if you followed Miss Baxter's path correctly.

PUZZLE 15

The letters in this star form a very familiar series. Which letter would you place in the middle? If you choose T, go to 3. If you choose M, go to 11. If you choose S, go to 13.

The St Swithin's (Wednesdays) Scout Troop leader decided to set an initiative test. This is it. Can you follow the True Path to its end?

PUZZLE 1

Three of the following are anagrams of the names of famous statesmen. Which is the odd one out?

1) LEDAANM 2) INHDAG
3) NNEEYDK 4) PAPEL

If you choose 1, go to 11. If you choose 2, go to 7. If you choose 3, go to 5. If you choose 4, go to 10.

PUZZLE 2

Which number comes next in this series, replacing the question mark?

1   2   6   ?

When you have the answer add 3 and go to the next location.

PUZZLE 3

Which letter comes next in this series, and will replace the question mark?

J A S O N ?

If you choose N, go to 11. If you choose D, go to 15. If you choose G, go to 9.

PUZZLE 4

Which of the following symbols is the odd one out?

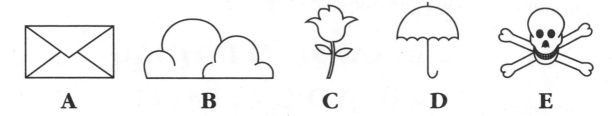

A   B   C   D   E

If you choose A, go to 3. If you choose B, go to 12. If you choose C, go to 9. If you choose D, go to 2. If you choose E, go to 7.

PUZZLE 5

Which numbers will the hands of the fourth clock, above, point to? When you have the two numbers add them together, add 2, and go to the next location.

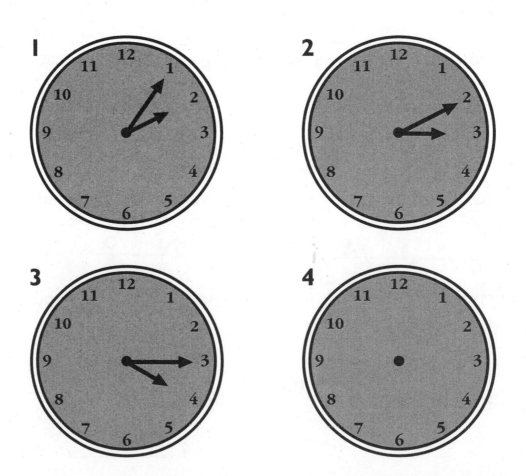

PUZZLE 6

The following letters relate to heavenly bodies. Which one is missing and will replace the question mark?

M V E M J S U N ?

If you choose A, go to 14, If you choose M, go to 12. If you choose P, go to 9.

PUZZLE 7

Which of the following cubes is the odd one out? If you choose A, go to 11. If you choose B, go to 8. If you choose C, go to 10. If you choose E, go to 2.

PUZZLE 8

Which letter will complete this series and replace the question mark?

S   S   F   T   W   T   ?

If you choose M, go to 12. If you choose Y, go to 4. If you choose L, go to 7.

PUZZLE 9

Which number comes next in this series, replacing the question mark?

12   21   36   63   45   ?

54

When you have the answer, subtract 40 and go to the next location.

PUZZLE 10

Which letter is needed to complete the diagram below? If you choose K, go to 3. If you choose G, go to 9. If you choose I, go to 8.

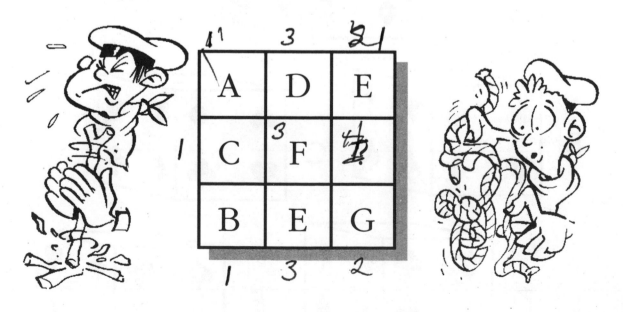

PUZZLE 11

Find a letter to replace the question mark. If you choose X, go to 14. If you choose K, go to 9. If you choose N, go to 6.

O	T	T
S	F	F
S	E	?

PUZZLE 12

Which letter is needed to complete the diagram below? If you choose A, go to 14. If you choose R, go to 4. If you choose Q, go to 15.

Z	U	T
Y	V	S
X	W	?

PUZZLE 13

These crates are marked with their destination. Which is the odd one out? If you choose A, go to 6. If you choose B, go to 12. If you choose C, go to 3.

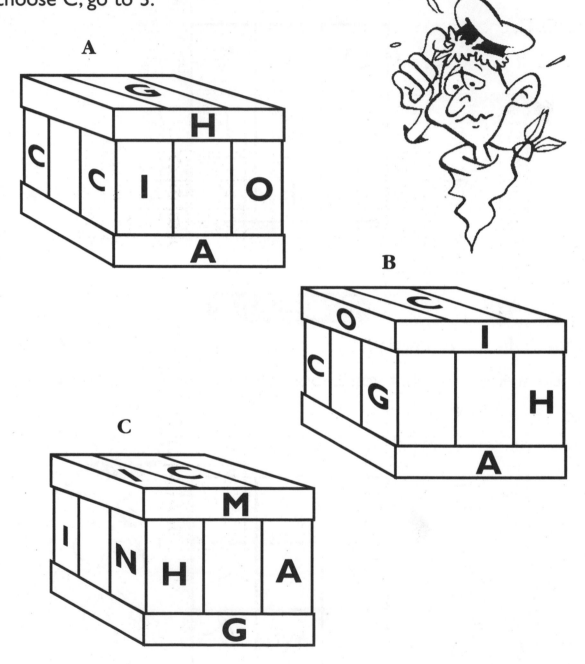

A

B

C

PUZZLE 14

Which square of nine letters should replace the one that's missing? The first letter is A at the top left corner, and the series runs in a diagonal zigzag with the order A, B, C, A, A, B, B, C, C, A, A, A, B, B, B, C, C, C, until you reach the bottom right corner. If you choose A, go to 16. If you choose B, go to 2. If you choose C, go to 5.

A	C	A	A	A	C	A	C	A	A	B	B	B	B	C	A
B	A	C	A	B	A	C	B	C	C	A	C	B	C	C	A
B	C	B	A	B	C	C	C	A	A	C	B	C	C	A	C
B	B	C	B	B	A	C	A	C	A	A	A	B	B	B	A
B	C	C	B	A	B	B	B	A	A	B	B	B	A	A	A
C	C	B	B	B				A	C	A	B	C	B	C	A
A	A	B	B	C				A	A	C	C	B	C	A	B
A	C	A	C	C				C	C	C	C	B	B	A	B
C	A	A	C	B	B	B	B	C	B	C	B	B	A	B	A
A	A	B	C	B	B	A	A	B	A	A	B	A	C	A	B
A	B	C	A	C	C	B	B	A	A	C	C	C	A	B	B
B	C	A	C	C	C	A	A	C	C	C	C	C	B	B	C
A	C	A	C	A	A	B	B	C	B	A	C	C	A	C	C
B	A	B	A	A	B	A	A	B	B	B	C	A	A	B	C
A	B	B	C	B	C	B	A	C	B	C	C	A	B	C	C
B	B	C	C	C	C	A	A	A	B	A	B	A	B	A	

A

B	A	A
C	B	C
B	C	A

B

A	B	A
C	C	C
A	C	B

C

B	B	B
C	C	C
A	B	A

PUZZLE 15

Which number should replace the question mark? Hint: The numbers inside each triangle will point you in the right direction. When you have the number, add 2 and go to the next location.

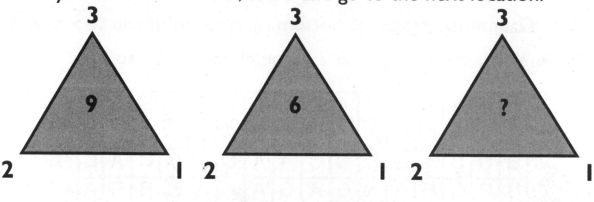

3   3   3

9   6   ?

2   1   2   1   2   1

PUZZLE 16

You have reached the end of this maze. Now check to see if have followed the True Path.

You have completed your Cadet year at the Intergalactic Federation Staff College on Xingeb V. Now comes the hard part. In order to get posted to active duty in the Federation Sat Fleet you must pass your final exam, a mind maze of great difficulty. Get this right and you are on your way to the stars! Fail, and your career is history.

PUZZLE 1

The number in the middle of the star is related to all those in its points. When you have the answer add 17 and go to the next puzzle.

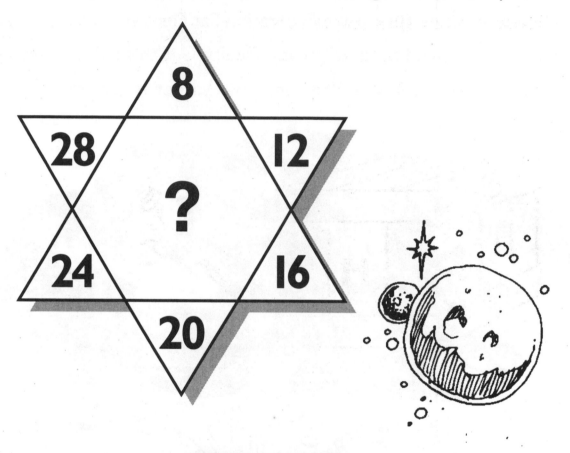

PUZZLE 2

What number should replace the question mark? Subtract 3 from your answer and go to the next puzzle.

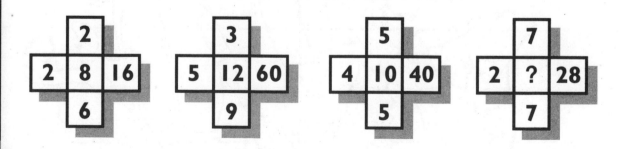

PUZZLE 3

Rats have broken into a warehouse on the lookout for a free meal. Which crate should they ignore? If you choose A, go to 17. If you choose B, go to 10. If you choose C, go to 9.

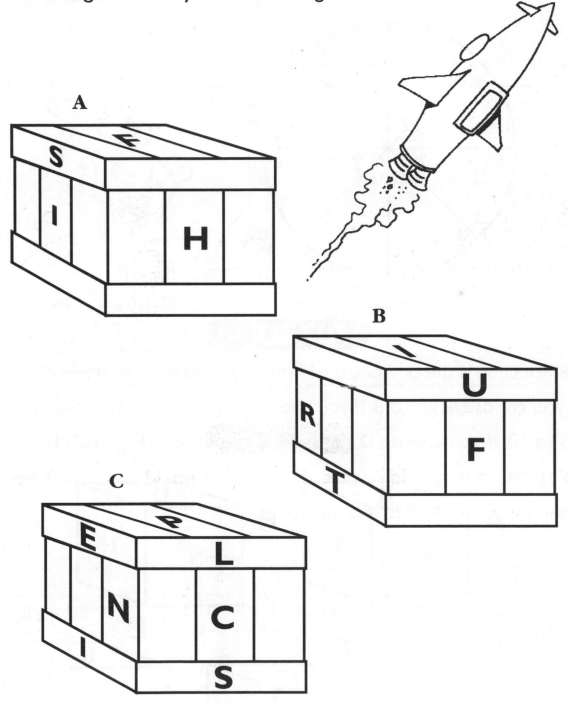

PUZZLE 4

Which number should replace the question mark? Hint: The answer may not be in the same segment. Subtract 15 from your answer and go to the next puzzle.

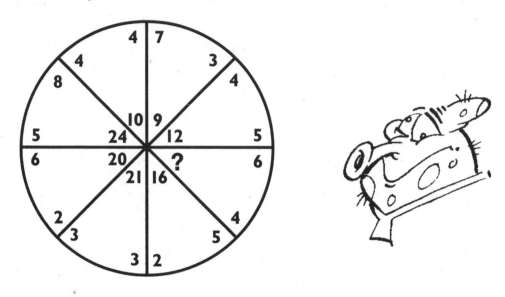

PUZZLE 5

Which cube is the odd one out? It helps not to think in straight lines! If you choose A, go to 8. If you choose B, go to 22. If you choose C, go to 10. If you choose D, go to 24. If you choose E, go to 11.

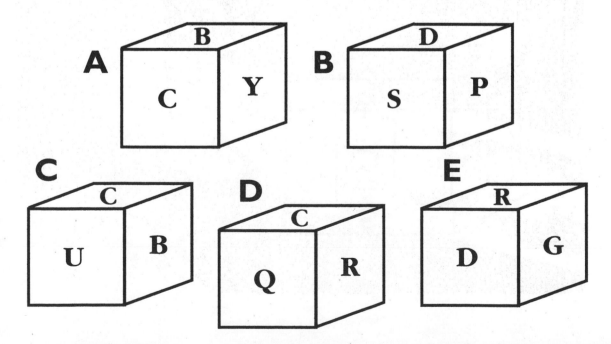

PUZZLE 6

Which number should go in the middle? When you have the answer, add 2 and go to the next puzzle.

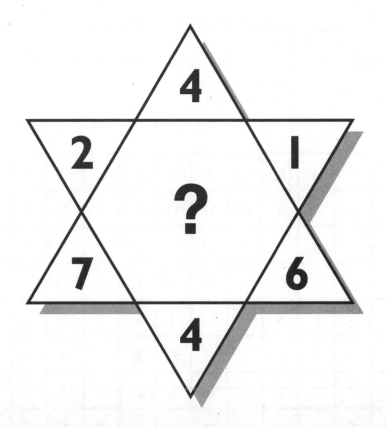

PUZZLE 7

The grid contains the names of nine pop stars and groups, written in straight lines, either horizontally, vertically or diagonally, forward or back. How many are written horizontally? When you have that number, add 12 and go to that location. The performers are: Guns N Roses, Michael Jackson, Elton John, John Lennon, Madonna, Seal, Take That, Wet Wet Wet and ZZ Top.

O	U	T	B	A	R	T	E	W	T	E	W	T	E	W	O
J	B	H	E	I	A	N	H	O	O	P	S	R	F	R	M
O	A	T	T	S	E	A	L	R	P	R	S	S	H	T	M
H	R	A	H	F	O	S	E	D	E	S	O	E	L	A	A
N	S	K	E	E	N	G	L	I	E	S	H	N	D	O	D
L	E	E	S	I	N	N	E	S	E	N	A	L	F	I	O
E	R	T	T	E	Y	A	O	S	E	D	I	E	R	T	N
N	N	H	A	R	M	R	R	T	O	B	N	T	O	H	N
N	D	A	H	O	N	E	V	E	N	S	A	E	S	E	A
O	R	T	E	S	E	L	T	O	N	J	O	H	N	G	E
N	U	I	N	T	D	A	S	I	L	O	O	F	O	H	O
T	E	U	D	O	N	E	L	Y	R	H	U	O	D	T	Y
O	G	M	I	C	H	A	E	L	J	A	C	K	S	O	N
T	E	N	I	N	K	Z	Z	T	O	P	O	F	O	N	L
H	U	D	E	O	O	G	L	R	O	N	T	E	S	O	N
I	R	T	A	N	M	D	L	A	F	E	I	H	T	W	I

PUZZLE 8

Find a letter to replace the question mark. If you choose F, go to 12. If you choose S, go to 18. If you choose B, go to 13.

Z	K	H
W	N	E
T	Q	?

PUZZLE 9

What is the missing number? Add 10 to your answer and go to the next location.

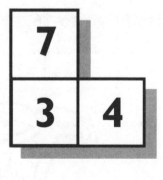

7
3 4

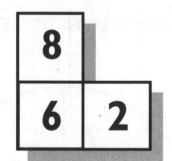

8
6 2

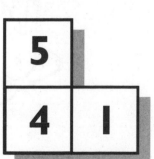

5
4 1

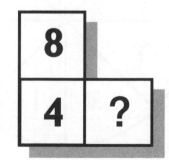

8
4 ?

MAZE 6

PUZZLE 10

Which cube is the odd one out? Add 21 and go to the next location.

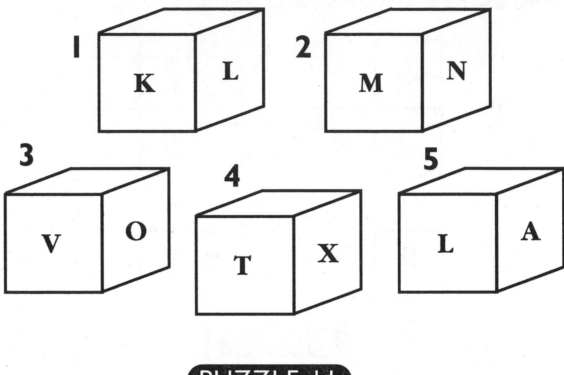

PUZZLE 11

What letter is missing here? This is a mystery worthy of the great Poirot himself! If you choose F, go to 16. If you choose H, go to 23. If you choose E, go to 18. If you choose N, go to 16.

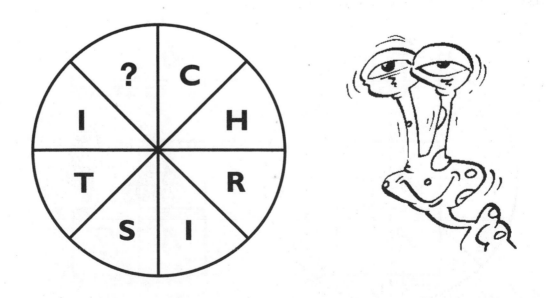

PUZZLE 12

What number is missing from the final box? Multiply your answer by three, and go to the next location.

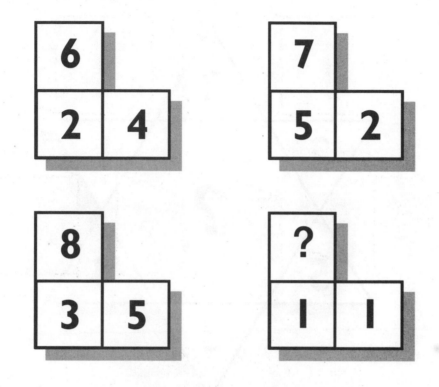

PUZZLE 13

Find a number to replace the question mark. Subtract 12 from your answer and go to the next puzzle.

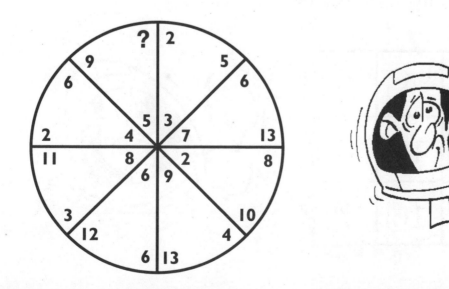

MAZE 6

PUZZLE 14

The missing number in the star is related to all those in its points. What is it? Add 14 to your answer and go to the next puzzle.

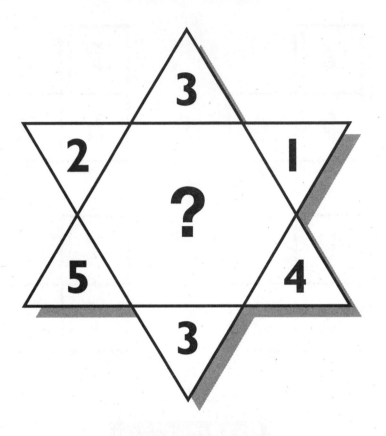

PUZZLE 15

Complete the numbers in the square. When you have the answer add 1 and go to the next location.

2	4	6
12	10	8
14	16	?

PUZZLE 16

What number is missing from the box? Add 14 to your answer and go to the next puzzle.

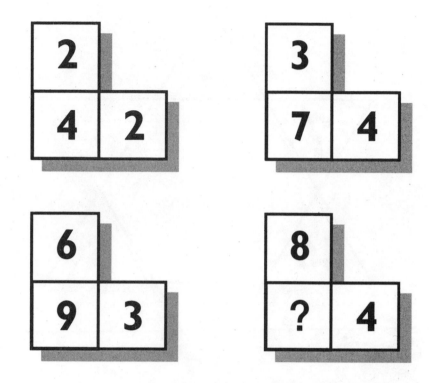

PUZZLE 17

Find the missing letter. If you choose Y, go to 22. If you choose D, go to 26. If you choose J, go to 21.

A	D	G
V	?	J
S	P	M

PUZZLE 18

What number is needed to replace the question mark? Subtract 13 from your answer and go to the next puzzle.

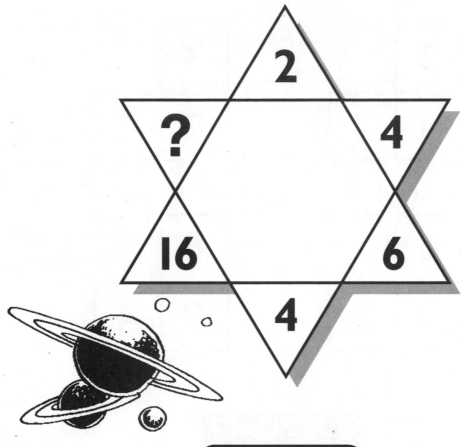

PUZZLE 19

What letter is needed to complete the final cross? If you choose B, go to 13. If you choose T, go to 3. If you choose K, go to 11.

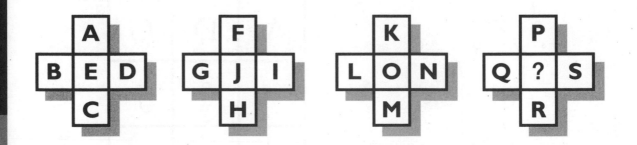

PUZZLE 20

What number completes the square? Subtract 32 from your answer and go to the next location.

4	8	12
32	?	16
28	24	20

PUZZLE 21

Find a number to replace the question mark. Hint: Think multiplication. When you have the answer, add 5 and go to the next puzzle.

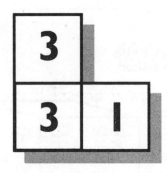

PUZZLE 22

Find a letter to complete the star. Convert your letter to a number based on its position in the alphabet, double that number, and go to the next location.

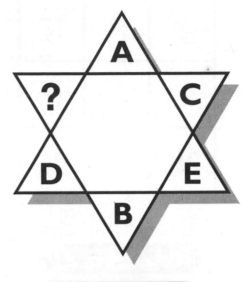

PUZZLE 23

Which is the odd cube out? Convert the letter of your answer into a number using its position in the alphabet, add three and go to the next puzzle.

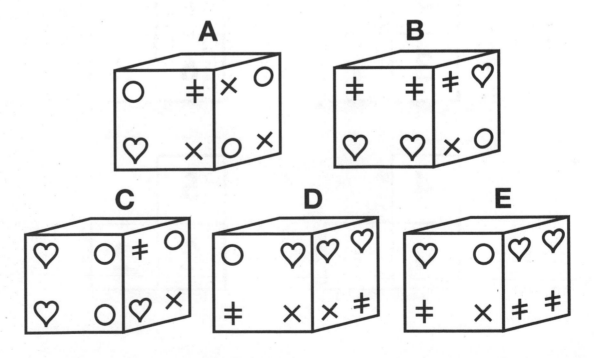

PUZZLE 24

Find a number to complete the last cross. Add six to your answer and go to the next puzzle.

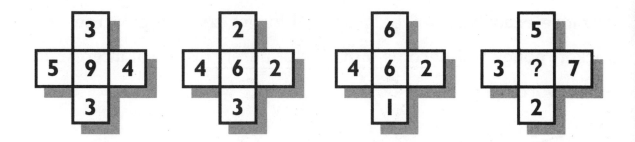

PUZZLE 25

Which cross is the odd one out? If you think it is A, go to 23. If you think it is B, go to 11. If you think it is C, go to 5. If you think it is D, go to 18.

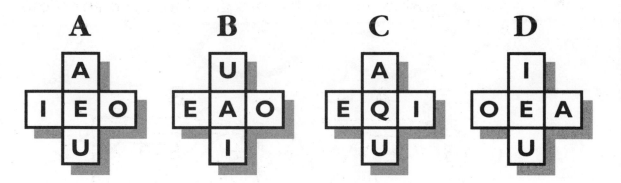

PUZZLE 26

This is the end of the test. Now look at your path. Add up all the numbers between location 5 and location 17. That is your final answer.

Your intensely ambitious parents have put your name down for the world renowned Einstein Academy for Precocious Little Tykes. You are not too thrilled but, should you fail this hideously difficult entrance exam, you will be grounded longer than an oak tree, and pocket money will become a matter of purely historical interest. In other words, get solving kid!

PUZZLE 1

Find a number to complete the square. Hint: Is this prime time? Subtract two from your answer and go to the next location.

1	2	3
11	7	5
13	17	?

PUZZLE 2

An infamous Russian lurks within the square. However, there is one extra letter that is not needed to make his name. What is it? If you choose R, go to 11. If you choose J, go to 21. If you choose N, go to 6.

R	A	S
P	J	U
N	I	T

PUZZLE 3

Which face completes the series? If you choose A, go to 24. If you choose B, go to 12. If you choose C, go to 6.

A   B   C

PUZZLE 4

Which figure is the odd one out? If you choose A, go to 25. If you choose B, go to 9. If you choose C, go to 14. If you choose D, go to 13. If you choose E, go to 7.

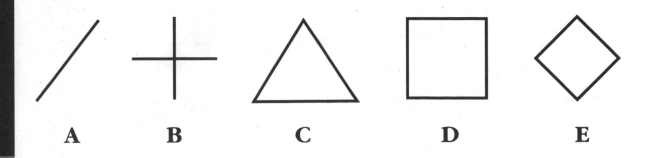

A   B   C   D   E

PUZZLE 5

Which face is the odd one out? If you choose A, go to 15. If you choose B, go to 9. If you choose C, go to 11. If you choose D, go to 16.

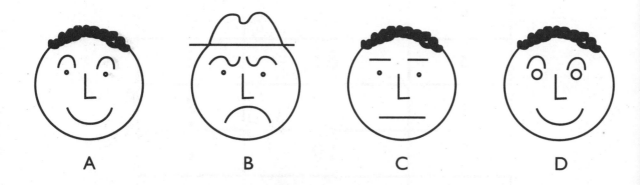

A   B   C   D

PUZZLE 6

Which number should replace the question mark? Hint: Try working diagonally across each square. From your answer subtract 25, and go to a new puzzle.

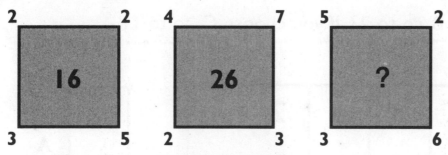

PUZZLE 7

Which number completes the final figure? Hint: The answer is *totally* in line! Take the number, add four and go to the next location.

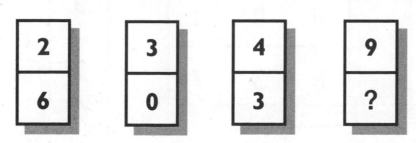

PUZZLE 8

Which number replaces the question mark? When you have the answer subtract 8 and go to the next puzzle.

4	54	5
3	63	6
7	27	2
9	19	1
8	?	2

PUZZLE 9

Which block completes the square? If you choose A, go to 12. If you choose B, go to 23. If you choose C, go to 11.

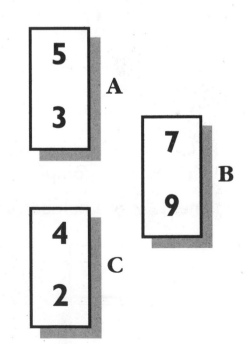

PUZZLE 10

Which letter comes next in this series? Convert your letter to a number based on its position in the alphabet. Then add 7 and go to the next puzzle.

A   E   F   H   I   ?

PUZZLE 11

Each of these pairs of scales is perfectly balanced. Use logic to discover which symbol is needed to balance the third pair. If you choose a square, go to 12. If you choose a circle, go to 15. If you choose a triangle, go to 22.

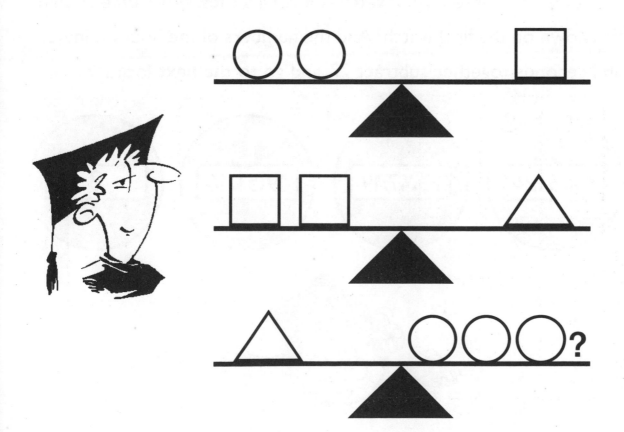

PUZZLE 12

These figures form a logical series. Which is the odd one out? If you choose A, go to 3. If you choose B, go to 14. If you choose C, go to 22. If you choose D, go to 17.

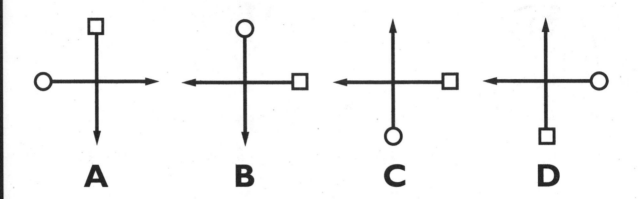

A   **B**   **C**   **D**

PUZZLE 13

The times on these digital watches form a series. What time should be shown on the final watch? Add the numbers of the hours, minutes and seconds together, subtract 77, and go to the next location.

3.43.24   23.47.19   19.51.14   ?

PUZZLE 14

These figures form a logical series. Which is the odd one out? If you choose A, go to 15. If you choose B, go to 19. If you choose C, go to 3. If you choose D, go to 22.

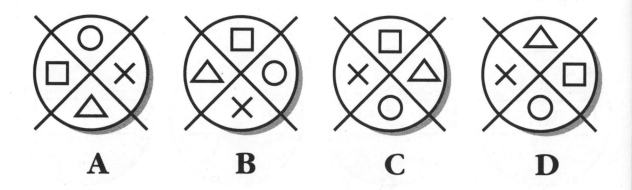

A   B   C   D

PUZZLE 15

Which matchstick man is needed to continue the series? If you choose A, go to 5. If you choose B, go to 7. If you choose C, go to 12.

A   B   C

PUZZLE 16

There is a logical connection between the times shown on these digital watches. What time should appear on the fourth watch? Add the hours, minutes and seconds together, subtract 62, and go to the next puzzle.

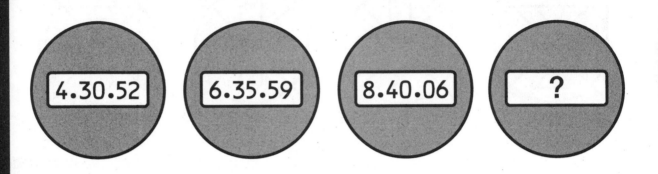

PUZZLE 17

Which figure is the odd one out? If you choose A, go to 16. If you choose B, go to 14. If you choose C, go to 18. If you choose D, go to 8.

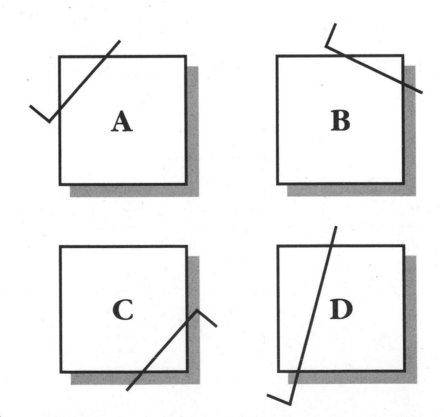

PUZZLE 18

The numbers surrounding these squares are all connected. Try to find one which will replace the question mark. Then subtract 43 and go to that puzzle.

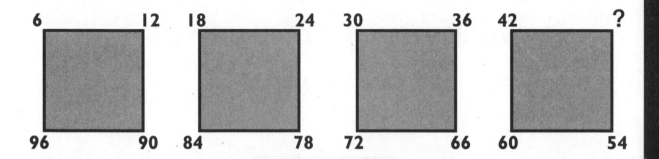

PUZZLE 19

These odd characters have lost their vowels. Try to discover which is the odd one out. If you choose A, go to 12. If you choose B, go to 11. If you choose C, go to 22. If you choose D, go to 25.

A) DCKNS   B) KNG

C) CHNDLR   D) SCHWRZNGGR

PUZZLE 20

These words are all linked. One does not fit. Can you predict what it is? The number of your answer is the next location.

1) RAM   2) CRAB   3) SCALES   4) TOMATO

5) GOAT   6) ARCHER

PUZZLE 21

Three of these strange words, when decoded, represent pop artists. The other is a different sort of artist. Which is it? If you choose A, go to 15. If you choose B, go to 10. If you choose C, go to 5. If you choose D, go to 24.

A) RYTHMCS B) RMBRNDT

C) QN   D) MDNN

PUZZLE 22

This is the end of the path. Add up the numbers between locations 6 and 14 (inclusive). The total will be your final answer.

PUZZLE 23

Which number will replace the question mark in the right triangle? This is a real toughie. Hint: Look at the numbers on top of each triangle first and see how they relate to the number inside the left triangle. Go to the next puzzle.

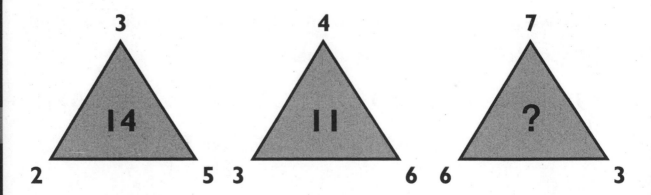

PUZZLE 24

Find a number to replace the question mark. This is a hard one so here is a big hint: Take a look at your 2, 3, and 4 times tables. Take your answer, subtract 13, and go to the next puzzle.

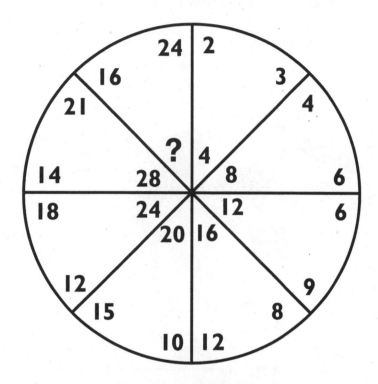

PUZZLE 25

Find a letter to continue the series. Hint: These look like letters, but think of them as numbers. The answer will have you thinking of a number. Add 9 and go to that puzzle.

N W H O I I ?

The Daily Globe has obtained tickets for a concert to be given by Tocsin, a new band that is just so amazingly cool you would give an arm and both legs to be there. Happily no major surgery is called for. The first person to solve the maze and send in their answer to the Globe's editor gets to see the show and meet Tocsin live!

PUZZLE 1

Find the next letter in the series. If you choose T, go to 15. If you choose L, go to 23. If you choose D, go to 12. If you choose M, go to 11.

A E C G E

I G K I ?

PUZZLE 2

There is a pop group hidden in the grid. Hint: Water music! When you have found them, go to the puzzle which is the first letter's position in the alphabet.

MAZE 8

PUZZLE 3

A strange signboard! It has nothing to do with geography. If we tell you that the vowels and consonants have different values, can you work out how far it is to Caen? Add 7 to your answer and go to the next question.

PUZZLE 4

Since 100 AD has a new century e.g. 200, 1000, 1900 and so on, ever started on a Sunday? If you answer yes, go to 30. If you answer no, go to 19.

PUZZLE 5

This grid contains the name of a famous river, plus one extra letter. What letter is left over after you have found the name? If you choose D, go to 20. If you choose S, go to 31. If you choose P, go to 17.

M	I	S	I
I	S	I	S
P	D	P	S

PUZZLE 6

If five equals 4, six equals 3 and sixteen equals 7, what does twenty-six equal? Hint: This isn't a magic spell. Add 18 to your answer and go to the next question.

PUZZLE 7

Which is the odd one out in this series? If you choose A, go to 30. If you choose B, go to 27. If you choose C, go to 13. If you choose D, go to 22.

A   **B**   **C**   **D**

PUZZLE 8

The boxes represent the gas, water and electricity services. You have to connect each service by a line drawn to each house. The lines must never cross each other, nor must they cross one of the boxes or one of the houses. How many ways of doing this are there? If you find more than 3 ways, go to 17. If you find only two ways, go to 29. If you find one way, go to 26. If you can't do it, go to 3.

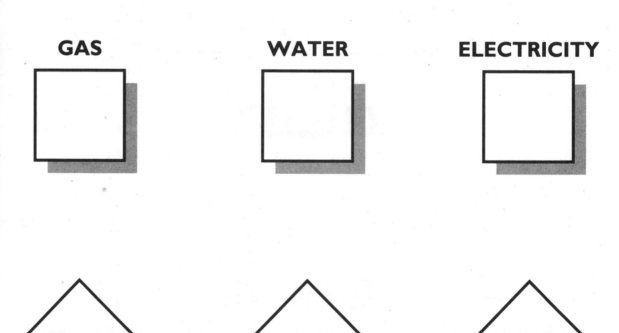

GAS   WATER   ELECTRICITY

PUZZLE 9

This signpost has nothing to do with real distances, but is based on the value of vowels and consonants. How far is Cambridge? Subtract 33 from your answer and go to the next puzzle.

PUZZLE 10

Each circle works according to the same strange logic. When you have cracked it you should be able to complete the final circle with a number. Add 14 to your answer and go to the next problem.

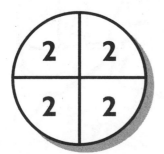  

PUZZLE 11

Scrooge was no fool. He saved the ends of candles, melted them down and made new candles out of them. If 4 ends would make a new candle, how many candles would he get in total when he had burned 48 new ones. Beware! This is not as easy as it looks. Your first answer is partly correct but you must think one stage further. When you have the answer add 9 and go to the next puzzle.

PUZZLE 12

There is an American President hidden in this grid. When you find his name you will see that we have added one extra letter. What is it? Convert your answer to a number based on its position in the alphabet. Halve it and go to that location.

B	C	I	I
L	L	L	L
N	N	O	T

PUZZLE 13

Find the odd one out. If you think it is spider, go to 17. If you think it is mantis, go to 23. If you think it is ant, go to 3. If you think it is cricket, go to 29.

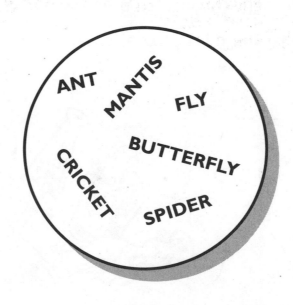

PUZZLE 14

Find the odd one out. Subtract 24 from your answer and go to the next puzzle.

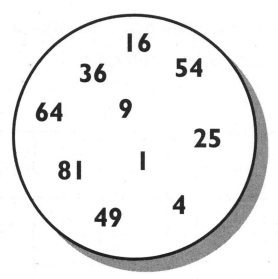

PUZZLE 15

A bottle factory melts down broken old bottles to make new ones. If they start the remains of 279 bottles, and they can get one new one out of three old ones, how many new bottles can be made in total. Beware! Even the new ones get broken, and you have to think this one right through to the very end. Subtract 131 from your total and go to the next puzzle.

PUZZLE 16

Three geographical locations are hidden in this grid. Which is the odd one out? Convert the first letter of the odd one out into a number based on its position in the alphabet, add 12 and go to the next puzzle

I	E	Y	E	A
U	S	T	I	P
A	R	L	O	A

PUZZLE 17

What is the next number in this series? Subtract 43 and go to the next puzzle.

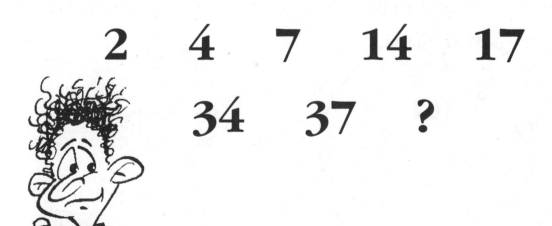

2   4   7   14   17

34   37   ?

PUZZLE 18

Which is the odd one out? If you choose cod, go to 12. If you choose herring, go to 22. If you choose whale, go to 26.

SHARK COD HADDOCK HERRING SALMON WHALE PLAICE

PUZZLE 19

Find the odd number out (which is actually a sort of hint). If you choose 102, go to 14. If you choose 131, go to 29. If you choose 72, go to 27.

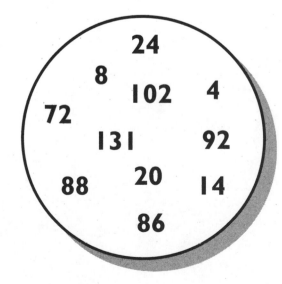

24 8 102 4 72 131 92 88 20 14 86

PUZZLE 20

This is a strange signpost. The distances are not geographical but are based on the values of vowels and consonants. Can you work out the distance to Chicago? When you have the answer subtract 19 and go to the next question.

26 ATLANTA
LAS VEGAS 31
26 ST. LOUIS
CHICAGO ?

PUZZLE 21

Scrooge has a thrifty habit of saving soap. From the remains of three bars he can make one new one. How many bars can he make, in total, from the remains of nine new ones? Add 14 to your answer and go to the next location.

PUZZLE 22

Which number would continue the series? Divide your answer in half and go to the next puzzle.

$$2 \quad 7 \quad 8 \quad 13 \quad 14$$

$$19 \quad 20 \quad 25 \quad ?$$

PUZZLE 23

Which is the odd one out? If you choose sun, go to 10. If you choose hurricane, go to 27. If you choose storm, go to 17.

TYPHOON

STORM   SUN

HURRICANE   CYCLONE

GALE

PUZZLE 24

According to the logic of this puzzle, would the number 10 go above or below the line. If you choose above, go to 4. If you choose below, go to 10. Hint: The actual figures won't help you.

$$\frac{1 \quad 3 \quad 5 \quad 7 \quad 8 \quad 9}{2 \quad 4 \quad 6} \quad ?$$

PUZZLE 25

Which number continues the series? Add 3 to your answer and go to the next puzzle.

1   4   8   11   15   18   22   ?

PUZZLE 26

Which number is the odd one out? Subtract 14 from your answer and go to the next question.

14
63
35   56   42
70   21
49
23

PUZZLE 27

Which letter continues the series? Convert your letter into a number based on its position in the alphabet. Then subtract 3 and go to the next puzzle.

T   T   T   F   F
S   S   E   N   ?

PUZZLE 28

Old Scrooge recycles blunt and used wax crayons. From 10 old pencils he can make a brand new one. How many can he produce in total if he starts off with 200 crayons? Be warned, you must follow the logic right through to the end. When you have the answer, subtract 8 and go to the next puzzle.

PUZZLE 29

How many squares of any size can you see in the grid? When you have the answer subtract 12 and go to the next puzzle.

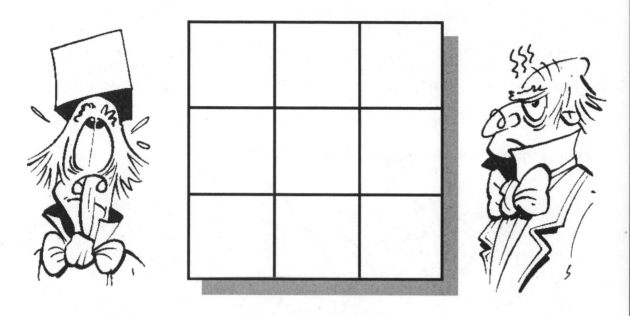

PUZZLE 30

Should the number 10 go above or below the line? If you choose above, go to 12. If you choose below, go to 10.

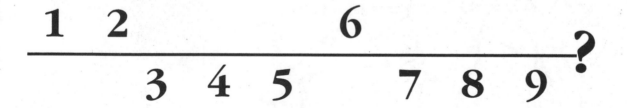

PUZZLE 31

This is the end of the Mind Maze. Now take all the locations between 26 and 27 (inclusive) and add their numbers together.

Are you still here? Do you seriously think that a mere child can pit its puny wits against a Maze Master such as I? You may have done well so far but now you're nearly right out of your league. This maze has 41, that's right count them, I repeat 41, of the most mind-bending, brain-busting puzzles you have ever seen. All linked into one intricate chain of mental mayhem. Get this one right and you will be a true Champion. Bet you don't!

PUZZLE 1

The flight numbers are in some way linked to the destinations. Which is the odd one out? It has something to do with initials. If you think it's Hong Kong, go to 17. If you think it's Paris, go to 36. If you think it's London, go to 24. If you think it's Bonn, go to 10.

FLIGHT 008 TO
HONG KONG

FLIGHT 016 TO
PARIS

FLIGHT 011 TO
LONDON

FLIGHT 002 TO
BONN

PUZZLE 2

Which letter should replace the question mark? Hint: In each square the letters progress through the alphabet missing a number of letters at each step. Convert your letter to a number in the usual way, add 9 and go to the next puzzle.

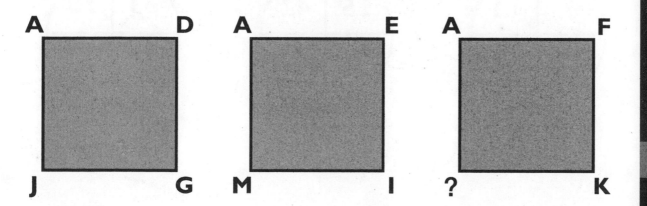

PUZZLE 3

The numbers in these diamonds obey a formula that involves adding, multiplying and subtracting the four outer numbers (in the same order around each diamond). Work out which number should go in the final diamond. Subtract 14 and go to the next puzzle.

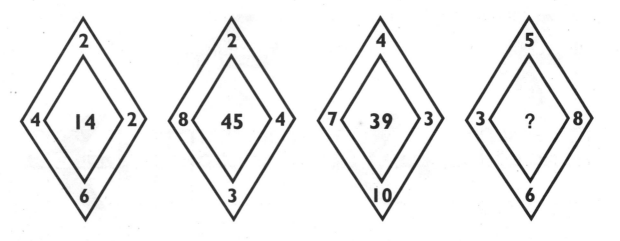

PUZZLE 4

Find a number to replace the question mark. Subtract 69 and go to the next puzzle.

PUZZLE 5

The grid contains nine concealed movie stars. They are: Helena Bonham Carter, Michael Caine, Cher, Clint Eastwood, Harrison Ford, Jodie Foster, Liam Neeson, Oliver Reed and Julia Roberts. The names are written forward or backward, and vertically or horizontally, but some change direction. How many are there with a change of direction? When you have the answer, multiply it by 4 and go the next puzzle.

O	N	E	M	I	N	T	H	E	F	O	R	W	I	I	K
D	A	J	I	N	O	S	E	E	N	M	A	I	L	E	D
Y	A	U	C	T	O	M	D	N	A	R	G	F	L	O	W
C	S	L	H	H	A	R	R	I	S	O	N	F	O	R	D
H	M	I	A	H	E	R	A	X	E	W	O	O	D	S	C
E	A	A	E	C	L	I	N	T	E	A	S	T	W	M	D
R	L	R	L	E	P	J	O	D	A	W	T	U	O	A	N
L	L	O	C	N	I	O	T	A	E	O	E	O	O	N	A
G	I	B	A	T	S	D	U	N	H	L	H	F	D	C	G
R	L	E	I	S	T	I	C	D	S	F	T	F	W	A	N
C	A	R	N	O	M	E	F	O	S	T	E	R	A	M	O
I	L	T	E	A	C	H	I	N	T	H	E	G	R	E	L
E	D	S	F	O	L	I	V	E	R	R	E	E	D	A	R
L	I	T	T	L	E	R	E	D	R	I	D	I	N	G	E
H	E	L	E	N	A	B	O	N	H	A	M	C	A	R	T
K	L	A	W	A	R	O	F	T	N	E	W	D	O	O	H

PUZZLE 6

Find a number to replace the question mark. Add 15 and go to the next puzzle.

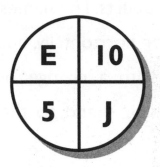  

PUZZLE 7

Which cube is the odd one out? If you choose A, go to 12. If you choose B, go to 39. If you choose C, go to 38. If you choose D, go to 16. If you choose E, go to 31.

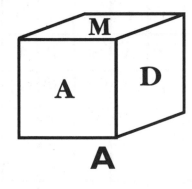 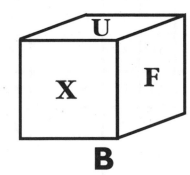

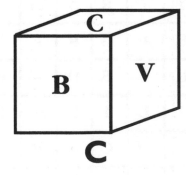 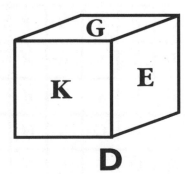 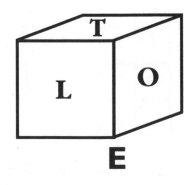

PUZZLE 8

Which letter would you move from the circle on the left to that on the right? Convert your letter to a number based on its alphabetic position. Subtract 2 and go to the next puzzle.

PUZZLE 9

Which letter would logically replace the question mark in this mathematical box? Remember that there is an easy way to convert letters to numbers. If you choose P, go to 20. If you choose F, go to 35. If you choose R, go to 36.

D	F	G
E	J	K
I	P	?

PUZZLE 10

The time these cars take to complete one lap (given in minutes and seconds) is in some strange way linked to the car's number. Which car is the odd one out? Add 20 to the number of the car and go to the next puzzle.

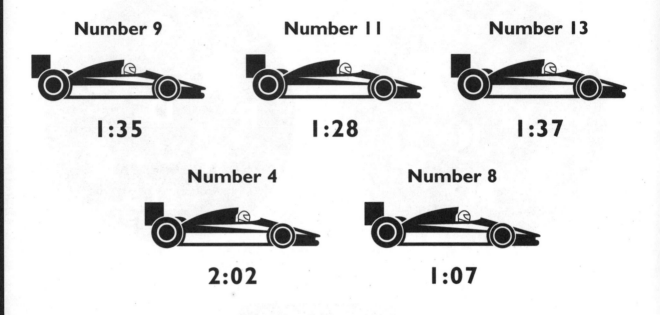

Number 9

1:35

Number 11

1:28

Number 13

1:37

Number 4

2:02

Number 8

1:07

PUZZLE 11

Find a letter to replace the question mark in this mathematical box. Remember that letters may easily be changed into numbers. Convert the letter into a number, add 10 and go to the next puzzle.

B	G	L
C	H	M
E	O	?

PUZZLE 12

Find a number to complete the final triangle. Subtract 10 from your answer and go to the next puzzle.

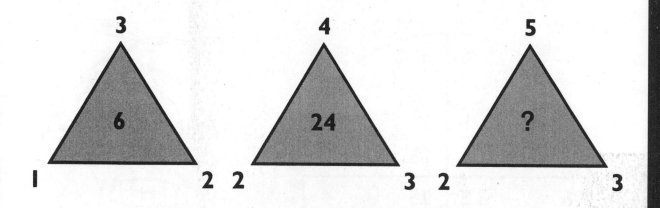

PUZZLE 13

Find a letter to complete the square in this mathematical box. Remember that letters can be used instead of numbers. Convert the letter into a number using its alphabetical position, add 15 and go to the next puzzle.

97

PUZZLE 14

Find a number to complete the circle. You need to perform a very simple calculation, but you put the result in an unexpected place. Subtract 3 and go to the next puzzle.

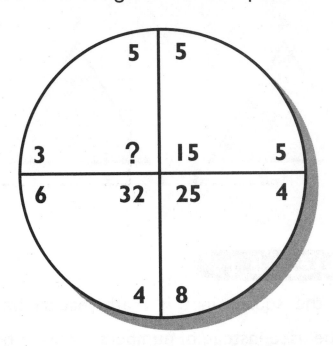

PUZZLE 15

Each number inside a triangle is the answer to a calculation involving one number from the outside of all three triangles. When you work out which number should replace the question mark, add 16 and go to the next puzzle.

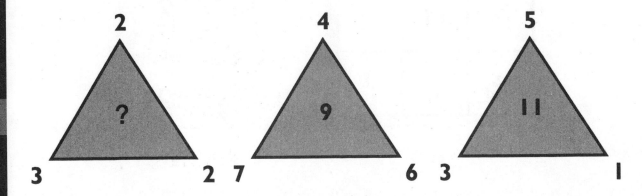

PUZZLE 16

Find the missing letter. Hint: Remember that you can write the alphabet in a circle. Convert the letter into a number, add 23 and go to the next puzzle.

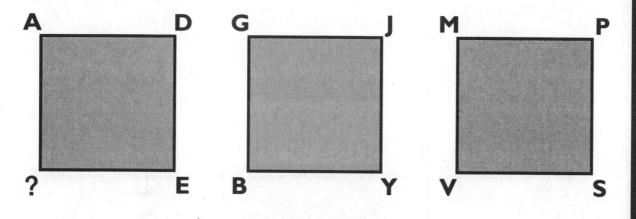

A   D   G   J   M   P

?   E   B   Y   V   S

PUZZLE 17

Using addition and subtraction of the hours, minutes and seconds, the drivers' numbers relate to the time they took to complete a race. When you have worked out the connection, you will see that there is an odd one out. Add 34 to this car number and go to the next puzzle.

Number 12   Number 11   Number 8

4:35:27   4:26:19   4:36:32

Number 7   Number 36

4:09:07   4:53:21

PUZZLE 18

Using multiplication and subtraction, the numbers outside each triangle relate to its central number. Which number replaces the question mark? Add 20 to your answer and go to the next puzzle.

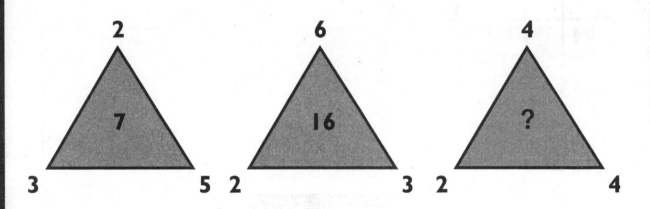

PUZZLE 19

Find the missing letter. You will find this puzzle quite easy if you imagine the letters of the alphabet going round in a circle. Convert your letter into its numerical postion in the alphabet, add 31 and go to the next puzzle.

PUZZLE 20

Find the missing letter. When you have it, subtract 17 and go to the next puzzle.

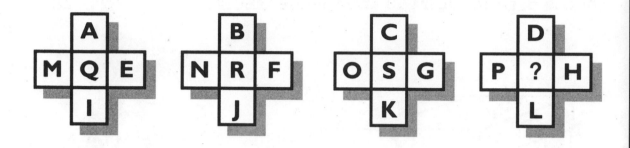

PUZZLE 21

Which number will replace the question mark in the star? Subtract 3 and go to the next puzzle.

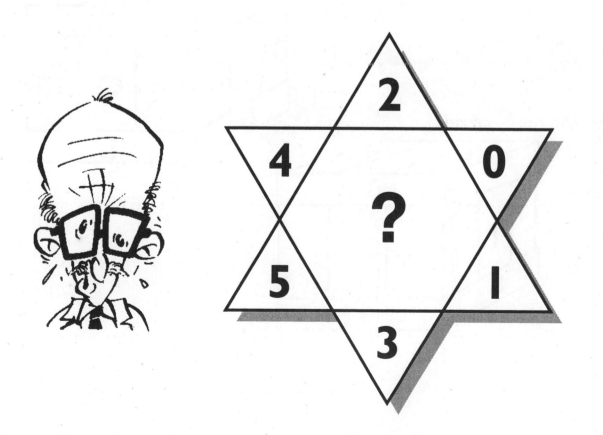

PUZZLE 22

Rats have invaded a warehouse. Which crate should they investigate most closely in search of food? If you choose A, go to 29. If you choose B, go to 28. If you choose C, go to 11.

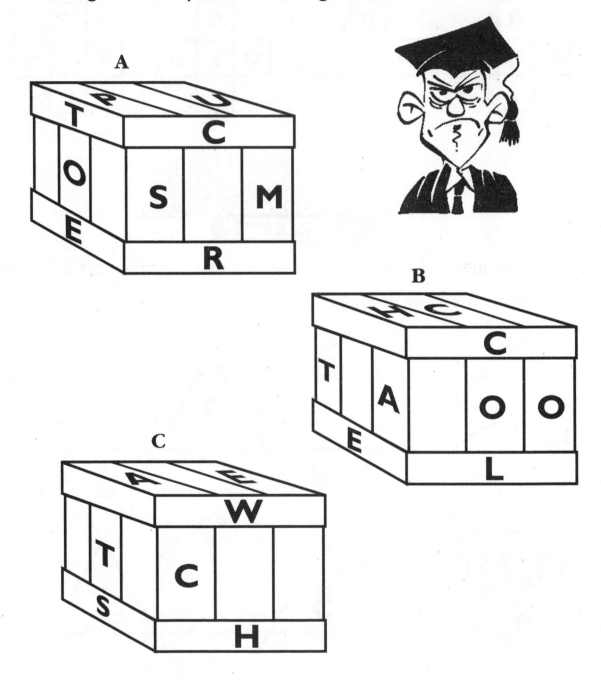

PUZZLE 23

Which is the number that does not belong in the triangle? Hint: Think multiplication. Add 8 to your answer and go to the next puzzle.

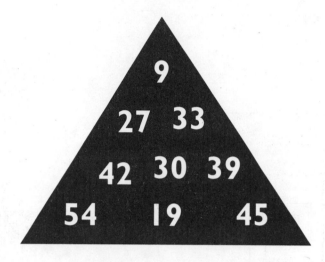

PUZZLE 24

The number in the middle of each sector is related to the numbers at the circumference of another sector. Which number should replace the question mark? Add 27 to your answer and go to the next puzzle.

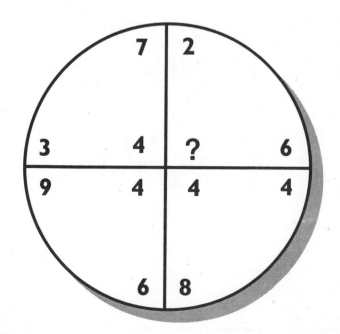

There is a connection between the house numbers and the people who live there. Which is the odd one out? Add 19 to the house number and go on.

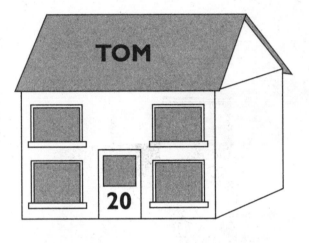

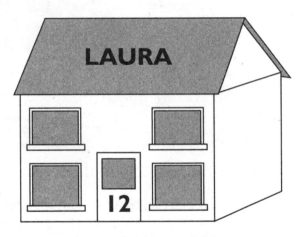

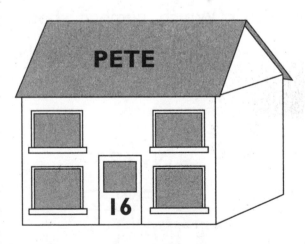

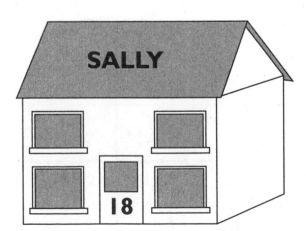

PUZZLE 26

How strange! All these farmers are called Brown, but in different languages. However, there is something even odder. There is some connection between the name and the number on the tractor. Hint: Sometimes endings are more important than beginnings. What number should Bruno have? Add up the digits of your number, subtract 8 and go to the next puzzle.

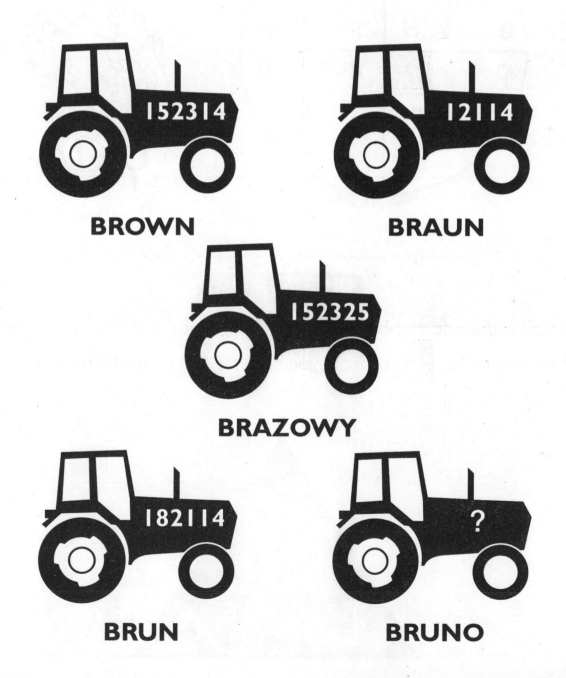

BROWN 152314

BRAUN 12114

BRAZOWY 152325

BRUN 182114

BRUNO ?

PUZZLE 27

Find the missing letter. Remember that letters are often used instead of numbers. Convert the letter into a number, add 2 and go to the next puzzle.

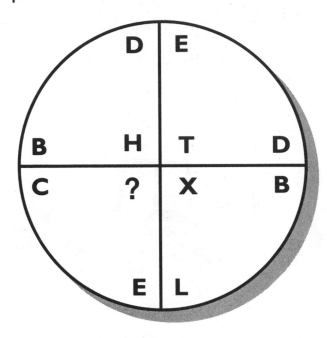

PUZZLE 28

Which is the odd number out in this triangle? If that isn't a clue, I don't know what is! Subtract 4 from your answer and go to the next puzzle.

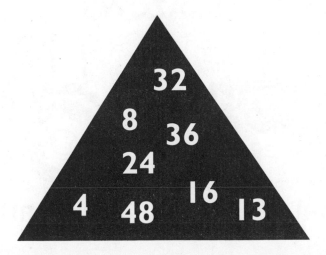

Find the odd one out. And if that isn't a clue, I don't know what is!

Subtract 66 and go to the next puzzle.

6
77   46
62
4   2
20
54   64
44

PUZZLE 30

These clock faces follow a simple logic. Can you crack it and find out what time is showing on the fourth clock face? Hint: A day has 24 hours. Add the two numbers which the hands point to, subtract 2 and go to the next puzzle.

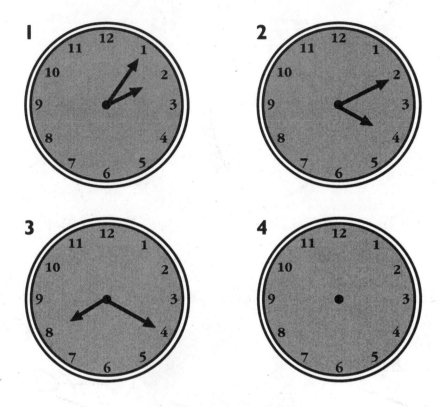

PUZZLE 31

Which figure is the odd one out? If you choose A, go to 41. If you choose B, go to 34. If you choose C, go to 18. If you choose D, go to 23.

A   B   C   D

PUZZLE 32

Which letter is the odd one out? Hint: Look for a country. Convert this letter to a number using its alphabetical position. Add 3 and go to the next puzzle.

PUZZLE 33

Which cube is the odd one out? Add 35 to your answer and go to the next puzzle.

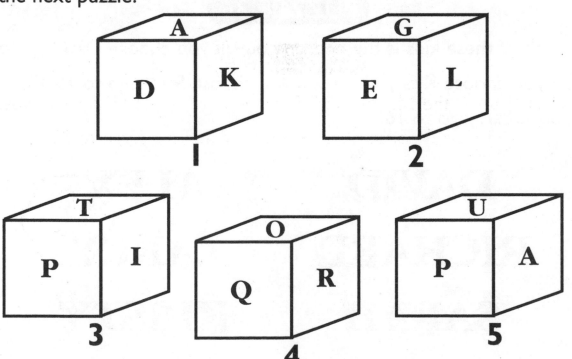

PUZZLE 34

Will the number 10 go above or below the line? Hint: think about the names of the numbers here. If you choose above, go to 27. If you choose below, go to 23.

$$\frac{1 \quad\quad 3 \quad 4 \quad 5 \quad\quad 7 \quad 8 \quad 9}{2 \quad\quad\quad\quad\quad 6} \quad ?$$

PUZZLE 35

Which letter comes next in this series? Hint: Try turning them upside down! Convert the letter into a number, subtract 8 and go to the next puzzle.

C E H I K O ?

PUZZLE 36

Which of these kids is the odd one out? If you choose David, go to 4. If you choose Kirsty, go to 5. If you choose Sarah, go to 18. If you choose Larry, go to 16.

DAVID   **ALEX**

RICHARD   **LARRY**

SARAH   **KIRSTY**

PUZZLE 37

Which month is the odd one out? If you choose January, go to 27. If you choose March, go to 34. If you choose April, go to 18. If you choose August go to 7.

JANUARY SEPTEMBER
APRIL AUGUST MARCH

PUZZLE 38

Which is the odd one out? If you choose Play, go to 12. If you choose Green, go to 22. If you choose Smile, go to 3. If you choose Cry, go to 19.

PUZZLE 39

The two boxes contain the mixed up names of famous people. Which is the odd one out? Take the first letter of the surname and convert it to a number. Subtract 2 and go to the next puzzle.

ANDRE	COSTNER
MICHAEL	GOODMAN
KEVIN	McCARTNEY
O. J.	FLINTSTONE
JOHN	AGASSI
PAUL	SIMPSON
BILL	JACKSON
FRED	COSBY

PUZZLE 40

How many months of the year have 28 days? Take two-thirds of your answer and go to the next puzzle.

PUZZLE 41

Congratulations, this is the end of the Ultimate Mind Maze! Now add the all the locations between 22 and 16 inclusive. This should give you the final answer.

DRIVEN MAD

Answer 1 is **A**, go to 5. Reading clockwise from the top, the letters spell Calcutta.

Answer 2 is **Yes**, go to 15. She dislikes places that contain the letter O.

Answer 3 is **O**, go to 14. Reading clockwise from the top, miss one letter each time.

Answer 4 is **12**. As the addition of S turns TEA, worth 4, into TEAS worth 8, S must be worth 4. Therefore, the addition of another S must make SEATS worth 12. 12 – 2 = 10.

Answer 5 is **D**, go to 7. The letters spell out Auckland.

Answer 6 is **No**, go to 11. She doesn't like people with two As in their name.

Answer 7 is **Yes**, go to 13. He does not like states with a T in them.

Answer 8 is **24**. Reading clockwise from the top, each number increases by 3. 24 ÷ 2 = 12.

Answer 9 is **37**. Reading clockwise from the top, add four each time. 37 – 33 = 4.

Answer 10 is **5**. Count left to right along the top row and right to left along the bottom. 5 + 1 = 6.

Answer 11 is **D**, go to 16. All the figures can be made with 3 lines.

Answer 12 is **D**, go to 3. The first three are anagrams of composers (Chopin, Beethoven, Mozart). The other is an anagram of Clinton.

Answer 13 is **N**, go to 2. The letters spell out Einstein.

Answer 14 is **I**, go to 9. Each letter corresponds in alphabetic position with the number above it. I is the 9th letter of the alphabet.

Answer 15 is **B**, go to 8. The letters spell Tom Thumb.

Answer 16
The Treasure Hunt takes the following path:

1   5   7   13   2   15   8   12   3   14   9   4   10   6   11

INTERGALACTIC TEST

Answer 1 is **S**, go to 13. These are the initials of the months of the year.

Answer 2 is **6**. Reading clockwise in each segment subtract the second number from the first and put the answer in the middle. 6 + 3 = 9.

Answer 3 is **6**. The numbers represent the number of letters between the corner letters, in alphabetical order. 6 x 2 = 12.

Answer 4 is **6.05.51**. The hours increase by one, minutes are divided by two and the seconds reverse digits each time. 6 + 0 + 5 + 5 + 1 = 17. 17 – 9 = 8.

Answer 5 is **20**. Starting from the top left corner, the numbers double at each step in a clockwise direction. 20 – 17 = 3.

Answer 6 is **8**. The numbers on the rim of each sector are added together and the answer is put in the middle. 8 + 6 = 14.

Answer 7 is **D**, go to 10. All the other squares are divided exactly in half.

Answer 8 is **U**, go to 15. In each row the letters form a continuous alphabetic series in the order: left, right and middle.

Answer 9 is **B**, go to 6. All the other circles are crossed by an odd number of lines.

Answer 10 is **14**. All the others are divisible by 3. The last seven puzzles you have done are: 12, 2, 9, 6, 14, 7 and 10, and the total is 60.

Answer 11 is **I**, go to 5. Reading across each row, miss two letters each time.

Answer 12 is **F**. All the others are vowels. F is the 6th letter. 6 – 4 = 2.

Answer 13 is **K**, go to 4. The letters spell Mark Twain.

Answer 14 is **Gondola**. All the words in the right circle describe sports. Those in the left circle describe forms of transport. G is the 7th letter, so go to 7.

Answer 15 is **Sesame**, go to 11. All the things in the left box can be eaten.

Order of Puzzles
If you answered the puzzles correctly, you should have worked through them in the following order:

1   13   4   8   15   11   5   3   12   2   9   6   14   7   10

SECRET AGENT

Answer 1 is **D**, go to 8. All the circles except D are divided into three parts.

Answer 2 is **0**. 0 + 15 = 15.

Answer 3 is **A = 12, B = 4**. Three-quarters of 12 = 9.

Answer 4 is **16 miles**. 5 + (5 + 5 [= 10]) + ⅒ of (10 [= 1]) = 16. 16 − 3 = 13.

Answer 5 is **13**. The numbers in the outside boxes, when added, give the central number. 13 + 1 = 14.

Answer 6 is **S**, go to 11. They form the initials of the first numbers and seven is next.

Answer 7 is **2**. 2 + 10 = 12.

Answer 8 is **45**. 4 x 3 = 12, 5 x 3 = 15, 6 x 3 = 18. 12 + 15 + 18 = 45. 45 − 35 = 10.

Answer 9 is **9**. The numbers on the outside of each sector are added to give the number in the middle. 9 − 5 = 4.

Answer 10 is **35**. The series increases by 7 each time. 35 − 33 = 2.

Answer 11 is **2**. All the rows and columns add up to 10. 2 + 5 = 7.

Answer 12 is **O**. The diagram lists the vowels in a zigzag. This is the end of the maze – now is the time to check if you have been pressing the buttons in the right order – see below.

Answer 13 is **20**. The numbers are written in order across the four sets of boxes. 20 − 14 = 6.

Answer 14 is **C**, go to 3. The letters on A and B spell Gorilla and Giraffe respectively (both are types of animal). The letters on C spell Monster (which is not an animal!).

Answer 15 is **T**, go to 5. The sum translates as 10 x 18 ÷ 9 = 20. T is the 20th letter of the alphabet.

Order of Puzzles
If you answered the puzzles correctly, you should have pressed the buttons in the following order to avoid an explosion:

1   8   10   2   15   5   14   3   9   4   13   6   11   7   12

CLASSROOM FUN

Answer 1 is **3**. Three States are written vertically: Indiana, Kansas and Texas. 3 + 3 = 6.

M	I	S	S	I	S	S	I	P	P	I	T	V	I	U	N
G	H	K	I	K	T	V	S	M	A	C	Q	R	N	T	K
C	B	A	L	R	X	O	T	Z	S	P	N	H	D	J	L
B	B	N	C	T	I	T	K	V	B	A	L	P	I	A	R
C	K	S	D	E	E	Q	B	L	P	S	R	S	A	C	I
B	O	A	B	X	E	D	I	R	A	G	I	A	N	N	T
C	A	S	S	A	B	D	R	O	A	H	V	B	A	N	T
D	V	W	Q	S	R	T	M	I	H	J	O	L	R	T	B
M	A	I	N	E	B	V	N	N	T	Q	P	M	L	H	C
X	I	C	R	S	B	R	P	C	I	R	A	M	A	R	C
A	U	D	R	A	O	R	E	P	D	E	O	M	O	R	D
A	D	A	T	F	E	R	I	A	R	I	Z	O	N	A	S
S	I	W	I	T	D	E	T	U	L	O	V	N	O	C	K
T	E	L	D	H	G	E	O	R	G	I	A	A	R	D	T
Y	A	T	I	X	E	L	P	M	O	C	D	A	E	R	O
C	E	N	I	G	M	D	P	A	L	A	B	A	M	A	Q

Answer 2 is **Go to nine**.

Answer 3 is **Two-ninths**, go to 7.

Answer 4 is **A = 8, B = 2.** 2 + 9 = 11.

Answer 5 is **C**, go to 14. The symbols repeat in the sequence **+ − × ÷**, which zigzags back and forth across the rows of the grid.

Answer 6 is **10**, go to Puzzle 10.

Answer 7 is **36**. 3 + 6 – 4 = 5.

Answer 8 is **3**. The numbers all increase by two if you start at the top left and work clockwise. Two-thirds of 3 = 2.

Answer 9 is **5**. The number at the top of each triangle equals the total of the numbers at the base. 5 – 2 = 3.

Answer 10 is **16**. The number in the middle of each square equals the sum of the numbers round the outside. 16 – 4 = 12.

Answer 11 is **W**, go to 8.

Answer 12 is **45 minutes**. 45 – 30 = 15.

Answer 13 is **2**. In each sector subtract the smaller of the outside numbers from the larger and put the remainder in the middle. 2 x 2 = 4.

Answer 14 is **52**.

Answer 15 is **S**, go to 13. The letters are the initials of the days of the week (Sunday is missing).

Order of Puzzles
If you answered the puzzles correctly, this is the path you should have followed:

1   6   10   12   15   13   4   11   8   2   9   3   7   5   14

SCOUT'S TRUE PATH

Answer 1 is **4**, go to 10. The first three are Mandela, Gandhi, and Kennedy. The fourth is an anagram of Apple.

Answer 2 is **10**. The numbers, spelled out, are all 3-letter words. 10 + 3 = 13.

Answer 3 is **D**, go to 15. These are the initial letters of months of the year from July. The missing month is December.

Answer 4 is **E**, go to 7. E represents a concept (the flag on a pirate's ship) but the others are all everyday objects.

Answer 5 is **large hand on 4, small hand on 5**. The hands advance by one at each turn. 4 + 5 = 9. 9 + 2 = 11.

Answer 6 is **P**, go to 9. They are the initial letters of the planets, and Pluto is missing.

Answer 7 is **E**, go to 2. The other four cubes have one of each symbol on both sides.

Answer 8 is **M**, go to 12. They are the initials of the days of the week (reading backward). Monday is missing.

Answer 9 is **54**. The digits are reversed at each turn. 54 – 40 = 14.

Answer 10 is **I**, go to 8. In each row the alphabetic position of the left and middle letters are added together and the answer, written as a letter, is put in the right column.

Answer 11 is **N**, go to 6. They are the initials of numbers, written as words, starting from one. Nine is missing.

Answer 12 is **R**, go to 4. The letters, reading backward from Z in alphabetical order, go in continuous vertical lines.

Answer 13 is **C**, go to 3. The letters on the first two crates are anagrams of Chicago. The letters on the third crate make up Michigan.

Answer 14 is **A**, go to 16.

Answer 15 is **3**. The numbers from the top of the triangles are added and put in the middle of the left triangle; the numbers from the left corners of the triangles are added and put in the middle of the middle triangle; and the numbers from the right corners of the triangles are added and put in the middle of the right triangle. 3 + 2 = 5.

Answer 16
The True Path is:

1   10   8   12   4   7   2   13   3   15   5   11   6   9   14   16

PASS-OUT POSER

Answer 1 is **4**. All the numbers are multiples of 4. 4 + 17 = 21.

Answer 2 is **14**. The numbers at the top and bottom are added together and the number on the right is divided by the number on the left. The answer to both sums is the same and it goes in the middle of the cross. 14 – 3 = 11.

Answer 3 is **C**, go to 9. A spells Fish, B spells Fruit, but C spells Pencils.

Answer 4 is **40**. The numbers on the outside of each segment are multiplied together and the answer is put on the inside of the diagonally opposite sector. 40 – 15 = 25.

Answer 5 is **A**, go to 8. It is the only one which contains a letter with no curves (Y).

Answer 6 is **8**. The values in opposite points all add to 8. 8 + 2 = 10.

Answer 7 is **5**. There are five artists written horizontally: Wet Wet Wet, Seal, Elton John, Michael Jackson and ZZ Top (see below). 5 + 12 = 17.

O	U	T	B	A	R	T	E	W	T	E	W	T	E	W	O
J	B	H	E	I	A	N	H	O	O	P	S	R	F	R	M
O	A	T	T	S	E	A	L	R	P	R	S	S	H	T	M
H	R	A	H	F	O	S	E	D	E	S	O	E	L	A	A
N	S	K	E	E	N	G	L	I	E	S	H	N	D	O	D
L	E	E	S	I	N	N	E	S	E	N	A	L	F	I	O
E	R	T	T	E	Y	A	O	S	E	D	I	E	R	T	N
N	N	H	A	R	M	R	R	T	O	B	N	T	O	H	N
N	D	A	H	O	N	E	V	E	N	S	A	E	S	E	A
O	R	T	E	S	E	L	T	O	N	J	O	H	N	G	E
N	U	I	N	T	D	A	S	I	L	O	O	F	O	H	O
T	E	U	D	O	N	E	L	Y	R	H	U	O	D	T	Y
O	G	M	I	C	H	A	E	L	J	A	C	K	S	O	N
T	E	N	I	K	Z	Z	T	O	P	O	F	O	N	L	
H	U	D	E	O	O	G	L	R	O	N	T	E	S	O	N
I	R	T	A	N	M	D	L	A	F	E	I	H	T	W	I

Answer 8 is **B**, go to 13. Starting from the top left corner, go down and up in a continuous zigzag. Jump three letters back each time.

Answer 9 is **4**. Subtract the bottom number from the top and put the difference in the box on the right. 8 – 4 = 4. 4 + 10 = 14.

Answer 10 is **3**. It is the only one with a round letter (O) on one face. 3 + 21 = 24.

Answer 11 is **E**, go to 18. The letters spell Christie (Agatha), the author of the Hercule Poirot novels.

Answer 12 is **2**. Add the lower numbers and place the answer on top. $1 + 1 = 2$. $2 \times 3 = 6$.

Answer 13 is **14**. The numbers on the outer rim subtract to give the inner numbers in each segment. $14 - 12 = 2$.

Answer 14 is **6**. Add opposite pairs of numbers. All totals add up to 6. $6 + 14 = 20$.

Answer 15 is **18**. A simple arithmetical progression increasing by 2 at each step. $18 + 1 = 19$.

Answer 16 is **12**. Add the number at the top and the number at bottom right and put the answer at bottom left. $8 + 4 = 12$. $12 + 14 = 26$.

Answer 17 is **Y**, go to 22. Start from the top left corner and work in a clockwise spiral, missing out two letters of the alphabet each time.

Answer 18 is **36**. Reading clockwise from the top, the first three numbers are squared and the answers are placed in the point diagonally opposite. $36 - 13 = 23$.

Answer 19 is **T**, go to 3. The alphabet is written in the crosses in a spiral.

Answer 20 is **36**. Starting from the top left the numbers increase by 4 in a clockwise spiral. $36 - 32 = 4$.

Answer 21 is **10**. Multiply the top and bottom right numbers. Put the answer at the bottom left. $5 \times 2 = 10$. $10 + 5 = 15$.

Answer 22 is **F**. The letters form pairs that are consecutive in the alphabet. The members of each pair are put in opposite points. F is the 6th letter. $6 \times 2 = 12$.

Answer 23 is **D**. It is the only cube which does not have a face with two pairs of identical symbols. D is the 4th letter. $4 + 3 = 7$.

Answer 24 is **10**. The numbers at the left and right are added together and the numbers at the top and bottom are multiplied. The answer to both sums is the same and it goes in the middle of the cross. $10 + 6 = 16$.

Answer 25 is **C**, go to 5. All the others contain only vowels. C has a Q in it.

Answer 26
If you followed the maze in this order, you are on your way to the stars:

1	21	15	19	3	9	14	20	4	25	5	8	13	2	11	18	23
			7	17	22	12	6	10	24	16	26					

Your final answer is 104.

ANSWERS

EINSTEIN ACADEMY

Answer 1 is **19**. They are all prime numbers in numerical order. 19 – 2 = 17.

Answer 2 is **J**, go to 21. The other letters make up Rasputin.

Answer 3 is **A**, go 24. The faces gain two elements at each step.

Answer 4 is **E**, go to 7. The figures gain one line at each step. E should have 5 lines.

Answer 5 is **B**, go to 9. It is the only one wearing a hat.

Answer 6 is **36**. Multiply the figures diagonally across the squares and add the totals together (5 x 6 = 30) + (3 x 2 = 6) = 36. 36 – 25 = 11.

Answer 7 is **9**. The number at the end of each row is the total of the other numbers in the row. 9 + 4 = 13.

Answer 8 is **28**. The numbers at either side are reversed in the middle. 28 – 8 = 20.

Answer 9 is **B**, go to 23. The numbers in horizontal and vertical rows are identical.

Answer 10 is **K**. Going alphabetically, K is the next capital letter composed of only straight lines. K is the 11th letter. 11 + 7 = 18.

Answer 11 is **Circle**, go to 15. The square is twice the value of the circle and the triangle is twice the value of the square, so the triangle must be four times the circle.

Answer 12 is **C**, go to 22. The figure turns 90° clockwise at each step. C disrupts the sequence.

Answer 13 is **15.55.09**. The hours go back by 4; the minutes go forward by 4; and the seconds go back by 5. 15 + 55 + 9 = 79. 79 – 77 = 2.

Answer 14 is **C**, go to 3. In pattern C, the square and triangle are in the wrong order.

Answer 15 is **C**, go to 12. One element is added to the figure at each step.

Answer 16 is **10.45.13**. The hours go forward by 2, the minutes go forward by 5; and the seconds go forward by 7. 10 + 45 + 13 = 68. 68 – 62 = 6.

Answer 17 is **D**, go to 8. It is the only one which does not cut a triangle off the square.

Answer 18 is **48**. The numbers increase by 6 left to right along the top row and right to left along the bottom. 48 – 43 = 5.

MAZE 7

122

Answer 19 is **D**, go to 25. With vowels added, the names are (a) Dickens, (b) King, (c) Chandler, (d) Schwarzenegger. The first three are authors, the other is an actor.

Answer 20 is **4**. All are objects connected with the signs of the zodiac except Tomato.

Answer 21 is **B**, go to 10. All the names are without vowels and spell: (a) Eurythmics, (b) Rembrandt, (c) Queen and (d) Madonna. Rembrandt was a painter.

Answer 22
Did you pass the exam? Here's the path you should have taken:
1   17   8   20   4   7   13   2   21   10   18   5   9   23   *14   3   24   19*
25   16   6   **11   15   12 and 22**

The numbers between 14 and 6 inclusive total 107.

Answer 23 is **14**, go to 14. Add the three numbers at the top of each triangle and put the answer in first triangle; then add the numbers at bottom left and put this answer in the second triangle. The three numbers on the right add to 14.

Answer 24 is **32**. Reading clockwise from the top, the first outer number in each segment increases by two each time, the second outer number increases by three and the central numbers go up by 4. 32 – 13 = 19.

Answer 25 is **E**. These are the second letters of numbers 1, 2, 3, 4, 5, 6. The next number is 7. 7 + 9 = 16.

TOCSIN TIME

Answer 1 is **M**, go to 11. In alphabetical order you go four places forward and then two back.

Answer 2 is **Wet Wet Wet**. The letters are jumbled up. W is the 23rd letter.

Answer 3 is **18**. The consonants are worth 6, and the vowels are worth 3. 18 + 7 = 25.

Answer 4 is **No**, go to 19. Amazing – but true.

Answer 5 is **D**, go to 20. The letters spell Mississippi.

Answer 6 is **9**. The number of letters in each number is spelled out. Five has 4 letters, six has 3 letters, sixteen has 7 letters and twenty-six has 9 letters. 9 + 18 = 27.

Answer 7 is **D**, go to 22. The number of elements increases by two at each step, but D increases by only one.

Answer 8 is **No ways**, go to 3. There will always be at least one line crossing with another.

Answer 9 is **48**. The vowels are worth 8, and the consonants are worth 4. 48 – 33 = 15.

Answer 10 is **2**. The numbers in each circle add up to 8. 2 + 14 = 16.

Answer 11 is **15**. 48 candles make 12 new ones but these 12, when burnt, will make a further 3. 12 + 3 = 15. 15 + 9 = 24.

Answer 12 is **L**. Bill Clinton is the name. L is the 12th letter. 12 ÷ 2 = 6.

Answer 13 is **Spider**, go to 17. A spider has 8 legs. All the others are insects, which have 6 legs.

Answer 14 is **54**. All the other numbers are squares (e.g. 2 x 2 = 4, 3 x 3 = 9, 7 x 7 = 49, 9 x 9 = 81). 54 – 24 = 30.

Answer 15 is **139**. At each stage the new bottles, when broken, will make more new bottles. 279 ÷ 3 = 93. 93 ÷ 3 = 31. 31 ÷ 3 = 10 (with 1 left). 10 ÷ 3 = 3 (with 1 left). 3 ÷ 3 = 1. Take this one and add the two others left to make another 3 . So, again, 3 ÷ 3 = 1. 93 + 31 + 10 + 3 + 1 + 1 = 139. 139 – 131 = 8.

Answer 16 is **Italy**. The others are Europe and Asia. Italy is a country, but the other two are continents. I is the 9th letter. 9 + 12 = 21.

Answer 17 is **74**. Double the first number, add three, double the next number, add three, etc. 74 – 43 = 31.

Answer 18 is **Whale**, go to 26. It is the only mammal; the others are all fish.

Answer 19 is **131**, go to 29. It is the only odd number.

Answer 20 is **26**. Vowels are worth 2 and consonants are worth 5. 26 – 19 = 7.

Answer 21 is **4**. He makes three from the original nine, and another one from the remains of the three. 4 + 14 = 18.

Answer 22 is **26**. The sequence here is add 5, add 1, add 5, add 1, etc. 26 ÷ 2 = 13.

Answer 23 is **Sun**, go to 10. The sun is a star, the others are all climatic conditions.

Answer 24 is **Above**, go to 4. The numbers above the line, when written as words, all contain the letter E.

Answer 25 is **25**. The sequence here is add 3, add 4, add 3, add 4. 25 + 3 = 28.

Answer 26 is **23**. All the others are multiples of 7. 23 - 14 = 9.

Answer 27 is **H**. The letters are the first of ten, twenty, thirty, etc., and hundred is next. H is the 8th letter. 8 - 3 = 5.

Answer 28 is **22**. Explanation. 200 makes 20, and from the 20 he will get another 2. 22 - 8 = 14.

Answer 29 is **14**. 14 - 12 = 2.

Answer 30 is **Above**, go to 12. All numbers above the line, if spelled out, are three-letter words.

Answer 31
Will you see Tocsin live? The path is:

1	11	24	4	19	29	2	23	10	16	21	18	26	9	15	8	3
		25	28	14	30	12	6	27	5	20	7	22				
				13	17	31										

The answer is 203.

ULTIMATE CHALLENGE

Answer 1 is **London**, go to 24. The flight number represents the alphabetic position of the first letter of the destination (eg, 008 = Hong Kong because H is the 8th letter). London is not the 11th letter.

Answer 2 is **P**. The first square misses 2 letters, the second 3. The final square misses 4 letters at each step. P is the 16th letter of the alphabet. 16 + 9 = 25.

Answer 3 is **33**. Add the figure at the top to the one on the right, then multiply the answer by the one on the left. Take that answer and subtract the figure at the bottom from it and put the answer in the middle. 33 - 14 = 19.

Answer 4 is **84**. Reading clockwise from the top left of each circle (left to right) numbers increase by 7. 84 - 69 = 15.

Answer 5 is **3**. The stars are: Helena Bonham Carter, Clint Eastwood and Jodie Foster. (See next page for grid.) 3 x 4 = 12.

Answer 6 is **17**. Each letter is above or below a number denoting its position in the alphabet. 17 + 15 = 32.

Answer 7 is **C**, go to 38. It is the only cube which has no vowel.

Answer 5

O	N	E	M	I	N	T	H	E	F	O	R	W	I	I	K
D	A	J	I	N	O	S	E	E	N	M	A	I	L	E	D
Y	A	U	C	T	O	M	D	N	A	R	G	F	L	O	W
C	S	L	H	H	A	R	R	I	S	O	N	F	O	R	D
H	M	I	A	H	E	R	A	X	E	W	O	O	D	S	C
E	A	A	E	C	L	I	N	T	E	A	S	T	W	M	D
R	L	R	L	E	P	J	O	D	A	W	T	U	O	A	N
L	L	O	C	N	I	O	T	A	E	O	E	O	O	N	A
G	I	B	A	T	S	D	U	N	H	L	H	F	D	C	G
R	L	E	I	S	T	I	C	D	S	F	T	F	W	A	N
C	A	R	N	O	M	E	F	O	S	T	E	R	A	M	O
I	L	T	E	A	C	H	I	N	T	H	E	G	R	E	L
E	D	S	F	O	L	I	V	E	R	R	E	E	D	A	R
L	I	T	T	L	E	R	E	D	R	I	D	I	N	G	E
H	E	L	E	N	A	B	O	N	H	A	M	C	A	R	T
K	L	A	W	A	R	O	F	T	N	E	W	D	O	O	H

Answer 8 is **O**. The left circle contains straight line letters, the right has curved line letters. O is the 15th letter. 15 – 2 = 13.

Answer 9 is **R**, go to 36. Convert the letters using their alphabetic position. In each column, add the top letter to the middle to give the one at the bottom.

Answer 10 is **Number 13**. Add all the digits in the time together to give the car's number. It does not work for No. 13 (it should be 11). 13 + 20 = 33.

Answer 11 is **Y**. The top row added to the central row gives the bottom row. Y is the 25th letter. 25 + 10 = 35.

Answer 12 is **30**. Multiply all three numbers around the triangle and put the answer in the middle. 30 – 10 = 20.

Answer 13 is **K**. In each row subtract the value of the middle letter from the left letter to get the right letter. K is the 11th letter. 11 + 15 = 26.

Answer 14 is **24**. Multiply the two out number in each segment and put the answer in the middle of the next sector, reading clockwise. 24 - 3 = 21.

Answer 15 is **13**. Add the three top numbers and put the answer in the right triangle; add the three right numbers and put the answer in the middle triangle; and add the three left numbers and put the answer in the left triangle. 13 + 16 = 29.

Answer 16 is **H**. Reading left to right along the top, every third letter is supplied and the series continues reading right to left along the bottom. H is the 8th letter. 8 + 23 = 31.

Answer 17 is **Number 7**. Add the hours and the minutes and subtract the seconds. The odd one out should be car 6 (4 + 9 (13) - 7 = 6). 7 + 34 = 41.

Answer 18 is **14**. Multiply the top and right numbers, then subtract the left number from this answer and put the new answer in the middle. 14 + 20 = 34.

Answer 19 is **H**. Reading from left to right move on six letters across each row. H is the 8th letter. 8 + 31 = 39.

Answer 20 is **T**. Reading each cross in the order: top, right, bottom, left, middle, the sequence jumps four letters at a time. T is the 20th letter. 20 - 17 = 3.

Answer 21 is **5**. All opposite points of the star add up to 5. 5 - 3 = 2.

Answer 22 is **B**, go to 28. It contains Chocolate; the others are Computers and Watches.

Answer 23 is **19**. All the others are multiples of 3. 19 + 8 = 27.

Answer 24 is **3**. Subtract the smaller number in outer part of each sector from the larger one and put the difference in the middle of the sector diagonally opposite. 3 + 27 = 30.

Answer 25 is **18**. The number represents the alphabetic position of the first letter of the person's name. Sally begins with the 19th letter of the alphabet. 18 + 19 = 37.

Answer 26 is **211415**. The number is the alphabetic position of the last three letters of each farmer's name. U is 21st, N is 14th, O is 15th. 2 + 1 + 1 + 4 + 1 + 5 = 14. 14 - 8 = 6.

Answer 27 is **O**. Multiply the numerical value of the two outer letters in each sector.

Convert the answer back to a letter and put it in the middle of that sector. O is the 15th letter. 15 + 2 = 17.

Answer 28 is **13**. All the others are multiples of 4. 13 – 4 = 9.

Answer 29 is **77**. All the others are even numbers. 77 – 66 = 11.

Answer 30 is **4.40**. Both the hour and the minute hands go to double the last number on the clockface, so the hour goes from 2 to 4, to 8, to 16 (or 4 pm on a 12-hour face) and the minute goes from 1 to 2, to 4, to 8. 4 + 8 = 12. 12 – 2 = 12.

Answer 31 is **C**, go to 18. The number of lines in the surrounding diagram corresponds to the number of elements in the matchstick figure.

Answer 32 is **K**. The letters form Canada, with K over. K is the 11th letter. 11 + 3 = 14.

Answer 33 is **5**. The other four cubes have only one vowel in them. 5 + 35 = 40.

Answer 34 is **Below**, go to 23. All the letters above are spelt with two vowels.

Answer 35 is **X**. All these letters are symmetrical about a horizontal line. X is the 24th letter. 24 – 8 = 16.

Answer 36 is **Kirsty**, go to 5. All the others have an A in their name.

Answer 37 is **August**, go to 7. It is the only one without an R.

Answer 38 is **Green**, go to 22. It is the only adjective.

Answer 39 is **Fred Flintstone**. All the others are real-life people. F is the 6th letter. 6 – 2 = 4.

Answer 40 is **12**. This is a trick question because every month has 28 days! February has 28 or 29 days and all the others have 30 or 31. Two-thirds of 12 = 8.

Answer 41
Are you a true Champion? Your final answer should be 303.
Path:

1	24	30	10	33	40	8	13	26	6	32	14	21	2	25	37	7
38	22	28	9	36	5	12	20	3	19	39	4	15	29	11	35	16
				31	18	34	23	27	17	41 = 303						